THE AFTERLIFE

FOR THE

ATHEIST

Gerry Connelly

Domra Publications
65 Constable Road
Corby
Northants
NN18 0RT
United Kingdom

First published by Domra Publications 1995

Copyright © 1995 G. P. W. Connelly

ISBN 0 9524417 5 6

British Library Cataloguing in Publication Data. A catalogue record is available from the British Library.

All rights reserved. No part of this publication may be reproduced or transmitted without the prior permision of the publisher.

Printed in U.K. by Centuryprint, Unit J, Cavendish Courtyard, Weldon, Corby, Northants, NN17 5DZ

CONTENTS

Page

Introduction	5
Acknowledgements	7
What You Will Not Find in this Book	8
The Sceptic	10
Other Proofs	11
The Near Death Experience	13
Explaining the Near Death Experience	19
The Electronic Voice Phenomenon	23
How to Experiment	28
In Company	35
Is it Safe?	36
Who are We in Touch with?	37
Further Experimentation	38
Behave Like a Scientist	39
Rational Explanations of the Phenomenon	40
How the Electronic Voice Phenomenon Compares with the Near Death Experience	46
Wisdom from the World Beyond	50
The Near Death Experience, the Electronic Voice Phenomenon and Religion	58
Reincarnation	60
Repercussions	63
Moral Troubles	69
The Way Forward	72
Appendix A: Comparisons with Spiritualism	76
Appendix B: The Science in *Breakthrough* – a Reappraisal	81
Select Bibliography	93
Index	94

By the same author, also from Domra Publications:

ERROL FLYNN IN NORTHAMPTON

INTRODUCTION

Some physicists have made the audacious and dangerous claim that they have almost reached the limit of physical knowledge: once the four forces of nature – gravity, electromagnetism, strong force and weak force – have been combined in their Grand Unified Field Theory, *everything* will have been solved. The last time such a claim was made, at the end of the nineteenth century, the world of physics was on the brink of being shattered by relativistic mechanics and by quantum mechanics.

   The truth is that as we approach the turn of another century, we are as far from knowing everything as our nineteenth century predecessors. All over the world, little things are happening that nibble away at the self certainty of scientific orthodoxy. A Dundonian plays around with gyroscopes and invents a device that can apparently defy gravity as well as Newton's Laws of Motion. Dowsing rods *really do* move when the holder walks over certain spots. These odd little aberrations must be allowed for when grand theories are formed, or eventually the little aberrations will bring about the downfall of that mighty theory. Much of the fringe sciences might seem eccentric, but some of today's mainstream theories – plate tectonics, evolution, even relativity – were also born outside of the law. And right in the middle of these embryonic fringe sciences are the numerous visions reported by people who have nearly died; and the strange voices that manifest themselves on magnetic tape when there is no one there to speak.

It is probably unfair to expect orthodox scientists to investigate these fringe sciences. Most are employed by people who already pay them to do other useful work. There have also been cases where orthodox scientists who have investigated fringe science areas have subsequently been "frozen out" by their colleagues. Hence many are rightly worried about their careers and their funding. The work in the fringe sciences must therefore fall to enthusiastic amateurs. There is nothing wrong nor unusual in this: in astronomy, for example, there being not enough professional scientists for the monumental tasks of skywatching; much work is undertaken by amateurs in homespun observatories, some of them schoolchildren. And excellent their work is, too.

The world has never before been so interested in fringe sciences. But, as the sceptical reader is aware, fringe sciences and pseudosciences are also attractors of all sorts of weirdos, cranks and frauds. Thus some respectable fringe sciences are trapped in the mire of Atlantis, crop circles as communications by aliens, astrology, religions who worship flying saucers, psychic crime detection, Nostradamus and other nonsense.

The study of what happens to the human when the body dies, thanatology, is one of these respectable fringe sciences, branches of which are respectable enough to be studied by orthodox scientists. However, much of the research into the possibility of post mortem survival has been done by those who claim to have supernormal powers, assisted by others who believe them. A sizable chunk of the public do not believe either that the researchers are supernormal or that they can contact the spirits of the dead. There are, however, other areas where those of us who are "normal" can research. This book will show you that not only can life after death be proved, but that this fact has been known for decades!

Furthermore, you can prove it for yourself by simple experiments you can perform with a piece of equipment found in most homes: a cassette recorder.

By contacting the dead, you can get some idea of what is *really* in store for us when we die.

Finally, I use the masculine as a common gender throughout this book. So what applies to he and him applies equally to she and her.

ACKNOWLEDGEMENTS

The author would like to thank all the people who have spoken to him in the manner described in this book, and have patiently answered his questions. Some identities are known. Some voices are recognised. Some will always remain anonymous.

The author also thanks Alan Sharpe for his suggestions on the book's format, and Gladys Reeves for her help with Appendix A.

The author owes a special debt of gratitude to Michael McPartland – wherever he is – the world's most underrated philosopher.

What You Will Not Find in This Book

This book is designed to stand up to the scrutiny of the atheist and the sceptic, the person who does not believe in a god or an afterlife, but who is willing to look at any evidence that might prove survival after death.

Many books that have hitherto been written on the subject of an afterlife have tended to rely heavily on the witnessed actions of the psychic medium. These books are sometimes written by a recently bereaved writer who goes to see a medium and is amazed by what he is told. "How could the medium possibly know that?" the author frequently asks. True, many mediums perform things that seem utterly impossible. But the likes of Paul Daniels and David Copperfield perform feats that are utterly impossible, too. But, since neither Daniels nor Copperfield make serious claims about having supernatural powers, we know that their feats are only tricks.

The truth of the matter is that there are sadly so many psychic quacks who prey on people when they are at their most vulnerable, that finding one that genuinely has the power to contact the spirits of the dead could be well nigh impossible. And, because of those same quacks, even if the medium was genuine, there would always be doubt in the mind of the bereaved person. For that reason, this book will not bear witness to any displays of mediumship.

You will not find religion in this book. Nor will you find scripture quoted as though it were irrefutable fact. I do not practise a religion, so I have no need to proselytise on behalf of any organisation. Besides, it would appear that what is in store for us when we die is not exactly what is taught by orthodox religion. Any religious person reading this book will probably have to do a little reassessing.

Another thing that often turns up in books on paranormal subjects is the question: "What does he have to gain by lying?" and "What motive could he possibly have for misleading us?" I know from my own life experience that the gain of attention is gain enough. I also know that sometimes the human being needs no motive at all for lying. There will be no statements like this in the book. Only one of the subjects covered by the book – the near death experience – is based on anectdotal evidence.

There are many annoying television documentaries these days that assume that telepathy, ley lines, reincarnation, auras and other goodies from the lunatic fringes of science and pseudoscience are as proven facts as the laws of nature. They're not. And this book will assume they're not.

Another annoying trait is the one where writers who write on paranormal, fringe scientific and pseudoscientific subjects quote from works of fiction or science fiction to support their case, as though these works of literature were hard evidence. In this book, fiction is only quoted to illustrate a notion, never to prove it.

Now I've dealt with what isn't in this book. I will get on with what is in it.

The Sceptic

Funny how the sceptic is always the villain.

The sceptic is the narrow-minded being who doesn't believe that witchcraft really works, doesn't believe that the horoscope in the tabloid really gives an accurate prediction of what will happen that day, doesn't believe that the next door neighbour was taken aboard a flying saucer and medically examined by shiny-suited aliens.

But wait a minute!

Why should the sceptic believe any of these things? The world around him doesn't consist of sorcerers who can turn the television set in the lounge into a snorting, foaming grey mare. When he kicks a football, the ball always follows a path predicted by Sir Isaac Newton. Small wonder the sceptic laughs when he is told that the rules and restrictions he lives by can be broken.

All sorts of strange people come into our lives with all sorts of strange claims. Are we *really* villains if we don't believe them? Suppose a man appeared on television and said that there were four Christs living in Jerusalem in the first century, and that Mathew, Mark, Luke and John covered a Christ apiece. Must we believe that? Would we really be ignorant people with closed minds if we didn't?

Of course not. So, instead of being a villain, the sceptic is the embodiment of reason, common sense and sanity.

So we can conclude that scepticism is a virtue.

I once had a teacher who one day in his class gave us some of his home-grown Mancunian philosophy. "For every virtue," he said, "there is a vice." He used the handling of money to illustrate his argument. To be generous is a virtue, but to be extravagant is a vice. Correspondingly, thrift is a virtue, but meanness is a vice.

My teacher's principle can also be applied to the matter of belief. To be open-minded is a virtue, but to readily accept any guff you hear or read is a vice. The same can be said of scepticism: to be sceptical is a virtue, but to ignorantly dismiss out of hand anything that doesn't fit the opinion you hold is a vice.

I would therefore say to the reader: be sceptical; the sanity of the world depends on it. But if you come across a piece of information that doesn't fit your idea of the way the world works, form a new view incorporating the new evidence, or strive to refute the new information; but never pretend it doesn't exist. There are far too many people who behave in the latter fashion; and, yes, some of them are otherwise eminent scientists.

Other Proofs
The most often used "proofs" of life after death are the ethereal worlds of ghosts, poltergeists, ouija boards, séances etc. Since this book is aimed at the atheist, the agnostic and the general sceptic, these matters will not be covered.

In the U.S.A., George Meek and Bill O'Neil claim to have built a machine called "Spiricom". This machine, say its inventors, can allow one to communicate with the dead more or less in a similar fashion to using a citizens' band radio. In a way, this project has many of the drawbacks of spiritualist mediums, and determining Spiricom's authenticity will not be handled by this book. It has not been so extensively researched as the near death experience; and, unlike the electronic voice phenomenon, to which it is obviously related, Spiricom can't easily be tried at home.

There remains one other "scientific" proof of life after death. In the *Fortean Times*, a journal devoted to fringe sciences etc., Ronald Pearson claims to have mathematical proof of life after death. Mr. Pearson's work is to try to marry the discrepancy between quantum mechanics, classical mechanics and relativistic mechanics by modifying the laws of Newton to incorporate quantum behaviour. His life after death idea is that when someone dies, he possesses more energy than had hitherto been thought; and, since this excess energy has to be accounted for, he moves onto the next life. Sounds fine. But is it proof?

My own understanding of quantum and relativistic mechanics is that they apply in *all* situations. The effects of relativity are as applicable to a courting couple strolling along the promenade as they are to a starship speeding towards Alpha Centauri A. But the effects of relativity on the courting couple are so negligible that both classical and relativistic mechanics approximately agree. In quantum mechanics, the same rules that apply to electrons also apply to double decker buses, but the effects on the buses are imperceptible. This makes the revision of classical mechanics seem like a futile exercise; but some good may yet come of it. Many scientists are unhappy about the illogicality of relativity and the hit-and-miss statistical approach of the Copenhagen Interpretation of quantum mechanics.

However, equations written on piece of paper are not in themselves proof: they have to have experimental evidence to back them.

The Near Death Experience

The modern investigations into the near death experience stem mainly from the research of the American psychiatrist Dr. Raymond Moody. While a student, he encountered a professor of psychiatry who had "died" twice within ten minutes and had had an odd experience while he was "dead". The professor of psychiatry was rescuscitated, and lived to tell his story during some of his lectures. Among the listeners was Moody. Later in life, when Dr. Moody had become a college lecturer, he heard another near death experience account from one of his students. Intrigued, Dr. Moody began to collect near death experience accounts. The result was his best-selling book, *Life After Life*, published in 1975.

In fact, as Dr. Moody himself found, the near death experience is not new. Several works, such as Sir William Barrett's 19th century book, *Death Bed Visions*, describes events similar to the near death experience. A work dating back to time immemorial, *The Tibetan Book of the Dead*, gives a description of what happens to the spiritual body after death that closely mirrors the near death experience. The work goes deep into death, concentrating on Tibetan notions of reincarnation. An even older work is *The Egyptian Book of the Dead*, again including many of the features of the near death experience. Both the Tibetan and the Egyptian books were written to be read out to the dying and the dead to help them find their ways in the world beyond.

So the near death experience had been noticed and recorded before. What has changed, however, is that modern medical resuscitation techniques are hauling people back from the brink of death more often. Hence more near death experiences.

There are several features common to near death experiences. Some of these are usually included in the recollections of the near death experiencers. Accounts of what happens to the experiencer between the point of death and the point of resuscitation tend to have *similar* features rather than being *identical.*

Common features are:

a) An annoying noise: ringing, buzzing, banging, howling.

b) A feeling of being out of one's body.

c) The vanishment of pain.

d) Seeing one's own body, often after failing to initially recognise it; and often from a point a few metres above the body.

e) Unsuccessfully trying to attract the attention of others in the vicinity: they don't respond to one's cries.

f) The discovery of one's spiritual (astral) body.

g) The realisation that the spiritual body can pass through walls, through people.

h) The appearance of a kind of tunnel, or staircase, or sometimes even a boat.

i) The travelling at rapid speed towards a light at the end of the tunnel.

j) The awareness – either before, during or after the journey through the tunnel – that one is in the company of other spiritual beings who are often recognised as relatives and friends who have died.

k) The appearance of a brilliant "being of light", who is accompanied by an intense feeling of love.

l) The replay of one's life, usually conducted by the being of light.

m) The announcement by the being of light that the experiencer must go back into his body.

n) The rapid journey of the spiritual body back into the earthly body to coincide with resuscitation.

The order in which these events occur can often be switched around. For instance, Dr. Moody's first book on the near death experience, *Life After Life*, has the tunnel incident between the moment of death and the leaving of the earthly body by the spiritual body. In later books he corrects this order and moves the appearance of the tunnel until after the earthly and spiritual bodies have separated so as to accord with the majority of his cases.

Once out of the earthly body, the spiritual body is often able to think more clearly. If the experiencer has been disabled during his earthly life, his disablities are gone.

The experiencer is able to see or hear everything that is going on in the room - and in any other room he cares to travel into. But "seeing" and "hearing" are the wrong words. Hearing is more like "reading" the thoughts of a person who is thinking of saying something before he actually says it. Seeing can no longer be the receipt of light on the retina. Some experiencers report all-round vision.

When the experiencer tries to attract the attention of others in the place where he has died, he might try to grab the arm of a doctor who is trying to resuscitate him. Either the doctor will ignore him or the experiencer's hand might go through the doctor's arm. Some experiencers feel something akin to an electric shock when this happens.

The scene at the end of the tunnel has been variously described as a bright - though not harsh - light, a pastoral scene, a flower garden and even - in the case of one child - a crystal fairy story castle.

The being of light is sometimes identified as Jesus or God or the Buddha or an angel. Communication is by thought transference, not

speech. This means that nothing can be hidden.
The replay of the experiencer's life on Earth takes place in an instant. The experiencer sees how both his kind actions and his careless actions have affected others. Sometimes an experiencer will recall that he felt everything felt by those affected by his life's actions, pleasure or pain. Note that this is not a grim reckoning. The being of light is kind and loving throughout and (thankfully) often displays a sense of humour. The being of light stresses that learning the ability to love one's fellow man and the acquisition of knowledge as the two most important things to have done with one's life, love being by far the greater of the two. The being of light often begins with the question: "Have you learned to love?" or "What have you got to show me?" Sometimes the life review is carried out by a "lesser being". Sometimes – especially in the face of a life-threatening accident – your life will literally pass before your eyes while you are alive.

All types of people have had near death experiences. These include children. In one case, mentioned in Dr. Moody's *The Light Beyond*, the experiencer is as young as six months, the near death experience being extrapolated from her behaviour in years to come.

In *The Light Beyond*, Dr. Moody features some statistics gathered by Gallup, which appear to show that as many as one in twenty people in the U.S.A. have had a near death experience. But it might be unwise to read too much into these figures.

Dr. Moody's original work, *Life After Life*, is

really the only work of interest to us. Any subsequent research, whether undertaken by Dr. Moody, or by anybody else since *Life After Life*'s publication, runs the risk of having been contaminated by the accounts of fantasists.

The sceptic will be only too aware of the sort of people I have in mind: the ones who have seen ghosts, flying saucers etc. True, many people who have had a genuine near death experience will have been inspired by Dr. Moody's original book to come forward and tell their story, after having kept it to themselves for years for fear of being ridiculed. But how many have come forward to seek attention; or, in some misguided way, to add their forged twopenn'orth to the pot in order to "prove" the life after death they believe in.

However, the near death experience is a genuine phenomenon: there are just too many cases around to ignore. What is more, the experience has a more profound effect on the experiencer than any dream or hallucination. Some near death experiencers claim to have had both hallucinations and near death experiences in their lifetimes; but the near death experience was nothing like an hallucination.

Furthermore, the feelings of love and peace are so strong that sometimes the experiencer, once resuscitated, will shout angrily at the doctor who saved his life. I personally know of one case where a woman called into the ear of a dying aunt: "Come back!" The aunt came back, but admonished her niece; she simply didn't want to return from the world beyond.

If the near death experience is neither dream nor hallucination, what is it?

Explaining the Near Death Experience

The rationalists have some fairly good explanations for the near death experience phenomenon.

The reason why the near death experience has to be treated differently from other forms of hallucination is that in case after case the experiences have been similar.

Similar. But not identical.

This would suggest that the near death experience might be more of a vision than something that has actually *happened* to the experiencer.

Dr. Raymond Moody has his own explanation. If a number of people went to France, they would each come back with a different tale to tell of their trip. That would explain why some people will be impressed with the feeling of love, some by the review of their life etc.

I don't find this explanation at all convincing. For example, the tunnel experience. Not everybody experiences the tunnel. The "trip to France" explanation doesn't work here. If an interviewer asked near death experiencers is he had been through a tunnel; some answered yes, some answered no. On the trip to France, how many American tourists would say that there was no aeroplane?

Although some experiencers who have had both a near death experience and an hallucination say that the two are different. But there is one form of experience that does resemble the near death experience: the out-of-the-body experience.

This is a phenomenon that can happen to someone on a sudden. But others – especially those who claim to be witches – say that they can leave their bodies at will.

Tests have been performed using people who claim to have self-induced out-of-the-body experiences. One experiment is where a multi-digit number is written on a piece of paper and placed on a shelf in the next room. The subject is requested to leave his body, find out what the number is and return to his body again. There has been some success with this experiment, the subject sometimes reporting the number correctly. Sceptics present pointed out that the subject might have seen the number reflected on the glass panel of a wall clock. This makes one wonder why this possibility wasn't eliminated before the experiment took place. Further experiments to find out whether the subject was reading the number from his bed or from a position in the other room have tended to point towards the latter.

A similar problem of explanation for the rationalist occurs with the near death experience. Experiencers accurately report what has happened to them not only in the room where their dead body was, but in other parts of the building as well. On one occasion, an American near death experiencer, who was brought to hospital with a heart attack, left her body and went outside the building. Outside she rose in the air and noticed a blue sneaker on the window ledge. After she had been resuscitated, she reported her experience, even telling those present about the sneaker. The blue sneaker was found exactly where she said it would be.

What most rationalists do when confronted with

this kind of evidence is to ignore it completely. This might be a good thing to do. What might begin life as a relative saying to a newly resuscitated experiencer: "I was in the next room and I was saying to Daisy: 'What's going to happen to poor Johnny?'" might turn into something slightly different by the time Dr. Moody gets to hear about it. The original story might become embellished: "I travelled through the wall into the next room. Iris was there, and she was telling Daisy..." Dr. Moody interviews Daisy. Lo and behold! The story checks out.

The following true story underlines the importance of objectivity at all times. An auditorium full of people was waiting for an audience with Pope John Paul II. The Pope entered. People began standing up, among them a man who had been sitting in a wheelchair. People around him began shouting: "A miracle! A miracle!" The faithful were jumping to conclusions. They assumed he was a paraplegic just because he was in a wheelchair. A rationalist would reason that many people in wheelchairs are perfectly capable of raising themselves: the man could have had a heart condition, for example. The truth was that the man was an able-bodied helper of a British party of disabled who had gone on a trip to Rome. He was sitting in a wheelchair belonging to one of his party because there was nowhere else for him to sit. The moral of this story is always look for a rational explanation first.

The rationalists have been trying to find plausible explanations for the near death experience. The prevalent theory they have come up with is that at the point of death, the brain – a kind of computer – runs the final programme. And this is what is happening to the near death experiencers. The tunnel the experiencers see is caused by random noise in the brain cortex. The tunnel with the light at the end; which can also occur in epileptic fits, drug trips and some migraines; can be simulated on computer. The feeling of being out of one's body can be duplicated by electrically stimulating the temporal lobe.* Other theories suggest that the whole vision is caused by endorphines or other chemicals being released in the brain.

So everybody is happy. A plausible theory has been found that fits all the evidence – well, nearly all the evidence. The fit is not exactly Savile Row, so those who believe that the near death experience is evidence of post mortem survival can continue to hold those beliefs. Since the near death experience takes place in the experiencer's head, if not his soul, there is a deadlock between believers and non-believers.

Those who advocate post mortem survival do, however, have some better evidence...

---

*This is a prime example of approaching the problem from only one direction. The rationalists have set out to rationally explain the out-of-the-body sensation. In so doing, they have totally overlooked an alternative explanation: that the separation of the earthly and the astral bodies is achieved by electrically stimulating the temporal lobe. This explanation, although admittedly less likely than the rational one, also fits all the evidence.

The Electronic Voice Phenomenon

The story began in 1959 with the Swedish film maker Friedrich Jürgenson. Using a portable tape recorder, he taped some bird calls on his estate, *Nysund*, in the remote Swedish countryside. When he played the tape back, he noticed voices that, so he thought, couldn't possibly have got onto the tape; because, at the time he made the recording, he was on his own. He went out and tried again. The voices had manifested themselves again. They were saying things about the birdsong and addressing Jürgenson. He tried to investigate this phenomenon further. He discovered that some of the owners of the voices he recognised, and they were dead. Jürgenson also tried recording the voices via medium wave radio with success. The fruits of his toil were published in 1964 in a book called *Rosterna från Rymden* (Voices from Space).

Among those who purchased a copy of Jürgenson's book was a Latvian psychologist, at that time exiled in Sweden, Dr. Konstantin Raudive.* Raudive, after a period of coaching by Jürgenson, began experimenting in a big way, collecting literally thousands of voices. In 1969, his book *Unhörbares Wird Hörbares* (The Inaudible Becomes Audible.) was published in West Germany. In 1971, an augmented version of this book was published in Britain and the U.S.A. under a more dynamic title: *Breakthrough*.

There was a minor brouhaha when the book was published and a few investigations into the

---

* The electronic voice (or electro-voice) phenomenon is sometimes referred to as Raudive voices.

phenomenon followed. Then everything died down. Publicitywise there has been little of excitement since the publication of *Breakthrough*. Today there are few that have even heard of this Cinderella science let alone practise it. Books written on psychic phenomena tend to ignore the electronic voice phenomenon. One book written to try to prove post mortem survival, Jeffrey Iverson's *In Search of the Dead*, based on a B.B.C. Wales television series, examines all sorts of psychic junk, while missing the only conclusive evidence of life after death: the electronic voice phenomenon is not even mentioned.

But I had heard of it. In the early 1970s, I read in a newspaper about a record that had been released containing samples of voices that had come inexplicably onto tape from people who claimed to be dead, among them Winston Churchill and John F. Kennedy. I made no attempt to obtain the record, but the subject interested me and I filed it away in my brain. In 1977, my bride and I were discussing life after death and spiritualism. She told me about a book written by a friend of her father's. This book followed the investigations into spiritualism by the Church of Scotland minister author following his wife's death. I found out the title from my father-in-law and called it up from the public library. On the back of the dust jacket was an advertisement for Raudive's *Breakthrough*. I called *Breakthrough* up from the library. I read it, and thought it was such an important book that I ordered a copy from a bookshop. The book then went onto the bookshelf, and from the shelf it went to the loft. In the meantime I was having science fiction stories published. In 1989, the British SF magazine, *Dream*, published my novelette, *Do Det Ike*, which I believe to be the very first SF story to feature the electronic voice phenomenon. In the story, my characters are faced with the problem of communication on the very first interstellar mission. Once the starship arrives at the nearest star outside our solar system, because nothing can travel faster than three hundred million metres a second, it will take four to five years for a message to go from one party to another. By way of a series of adventures, the story's protagonist comes up with the idea that interstellar communication could be achieved by way of the electronic voice phenomenon, using the entities who produce the voices as intermediaries.

In this story, I speculated that the electronic voice phenomenon was really all conjured up in people's imaginations, that there might be an imperfection on the tape and people would think it was someone talking to them.

My lesson was still to come.

My wife died. I was only forty; and, since longevity runs in my family, I might have to spend some fifty years without the woman I love. When my wife died, I was an atheist, and I didn't bother much about the afterlife, although I was aware of both the electronic voice phenomenon and the research into the near death experience. As well as my own grief, I also had an eleven year old son. How was the the loss of his mother affecting him? My copy of *Breakthrough* came down from the loft.

Much has changed since the days of Raudive's

book. The reel-to-reel tape recorders of the 1960s have given way to players of the Philips compact cassette, which has greater background noise as a price to pay for its practicality.

On the other hand, some of the basic hi fi equipment has become more sophisticated. In Raudive's day, one would have needed two tape recorders to copy a voice from one tape to another. Nowadays, machines with a double cassette deck are commonplace. The development of the radio/cassette player and the music centre makes recording from radio onto tape easy.

I tried some of the experiments in *Breakthrough* for about a week, using both radio and the recording machine's integral microphone. *Breakthrough* doesn't give very detailed instructions on how to conduct the experiments, although the direction in which to proceed is clear enough. During that first week I picked up nothing from the radio, and the integral microphone only picked up the whirring of the tape machine's motor. I got around the latter problem by fitting an external microphone to a battery operated dictaphone that took Philips compact cassettes rather than the mini cassettes used on most of today's hand-held dictaphones.

The first time I used this new set-up I heard nothing on the tape but the background hiss when I played it back. This confirmed my fears: if there were really voices out there, they wouldn't come through on an 11cm x 8cm x 3cm cassette recorder that was powered by two 1.5 volt batteries.

Like Raudive, I asked questions about death and about the afterlife, and I asked to speak to certain people who had died – my wife in particular. During my second session with the dictaphone and the external microphone, I asked the following question: "One hypothesis is that part of our bodies – the brain – exists in a fourth dimension..." Here I paused while I thought up the wording for the rest of the question: "...is this the part of us that survives when we die?"

The question was based on an idea that I had picked up from reading books on physics. One author – I forget which – had suggested that in a three-dimensional world, such things as thoughts and ideas are clearly non-three-dimensional. One reason for this could be that part of the brain was non-three-dimensional and existed in a fourth dimension.

When I played back this section of the tape I noticed what sounded like a grunt in the pause between "dimension" and "is". How had that gotten there? Was it me stammering? Was it a shout from the street outside from those returning from the night clubs in the early hours of the morning?

I played the grunt back again and again and yet again. The voice was male, had an educated English accent, and said very quickly: "No way!"

I played the voice to my son. He heard it, too. I played it to friends, relatives. Everybody heard it. I had received my first "grade A" voice. Now I knew what a Raudive voice sounded like, I was inspired to continue with the experiments, and many more grade A voices have manifested themselves on tape.

I now realise that I was exceedingly lucky to receive a grade A voice after only a week.

Raudive only succeeded after three months and he had been coached by Friedrich Jürgenson himself. Grade A voices are only a fraction of the total number of voices received. Most come in the grade B and grade C categories. Grade B voices are low murmerings that can sometimes be deciphered by hard work at listening-in. Grade C voices are background whisperings that will probably never be understood. At first, the untrained ear will hear only the rush of the tape. Once the ear has learned how to pick up the grade B and grade C voices, one can go back to the early recording sessions and pick up sounds that had hitherto been missed. My very first recording session with the dictaphone and the external microphone was not as fruitless as I had thought.

How to Experiment
This is so simple that it hardly merits instruction. However, there are one or two minor pitfalls that I can warn the reader of, which might speed up his success.

The first is attitude.

The entities you are contacting are people. Death has not robbed them of their individuality. They are under no obligation to reply. Experimenting with the electronic voice phenomenon is a serious matter. Because of these experiments, future generations may be able to hold easy, two-way contact with the deceased.

Therefore conduct the experiments because you want to prove to yourself that they work, because you would like to discover ways of improving contact, because you would like to improve the proof of the electronic voice phenomenon's existence, because you want to learn something about how the two worlds the living and the dead inhabit interact with one another, or because you want to contact someone in particular who has passed on.

The electronic voice phenomenon is not an oracle to help us make our own decisions. Above all it is not a party game nor a source of entertainment for yourself or for others. And don't even think about using it to find out tomorrow's horse racing winners or the winning numbers of the weekend's National Lottery!

Don't expect instant results. When you begin experimenting, your hearing will probably not be developed enough to hear grade B voices. You may be lucky and receive a grade A voice in your first recording session. Otherwise, there is no substitute for perseverence. As I have said, Raudive had to wait for months before he heard his first voice.

Once you have begun to receive voices, don't be downhearted if your pet questions remain unanswered, or the person you want to speak to doesn't reply. Keep trying. If you continue to be unsuccessful, it could be because the question you are asking is ambiguous. Or perhaps it can't be answered. Perhaps the entities on the other side are not permitted to answer it. If you suspect the latter, ask about it. Communication this way is slow and requires patience. Remember, before the tape recorder's invention, electronic communication with the dead was impossible.

Tape Recorders

As I found out by experimenting, price seems to make little difference as to whether equipment will receive voices or not, so long as it can take an external microphone. Owing to the simplicity of the equipment, you might get better results by recording with a monophonic machine. Price and sophistication mean little in the world beyond.

Ideally, you should use a reel-to-reel tape recorder. These have less background noise than the Philips compact cassette. However, it is almost impossible to buy one. And those that are available, for use in recording studios etc, are highly expensive. You might be lucky enough to purchase a second hand ex-B.B.C. machine. But, until more sophisticated recording equipment that can be used at home becomes available, one is left with the compact cassette. Fortunately voices do come through.

Microphones

As I have stated, integral microphones are useless so far as the electronic voice phenomenon is concerned. When buying external microphones, buy one with a long lead or buy an extension lead.

I possess two microphones, an expensive one and a cheap one. I can't detect any difference in performance; so you need not spend a lot of money on microphones.

Headphones

Stereo headphones are a necessity: most of the grade B voices can be heard only through headphones. If you are using a monophonic tape machine, buy a monophonic converter plug (a simple, cheap device, available from any high street electronics store) otherwise the sound will only come through one channel. There are also twin-channelled monophonic headphones for use with radio scanners.

Again, price doesn't seem to matter so far as quality of reception with headphones is concerned. The voices tend to exist in the higher sound frequencies (the treble), whereas, the most expensive headphones tend to be the ones with the best bass reproduction.

What has recently some onto the market is the in-the-ear stereophonic headphones with moulded speakers. The Philips SBC 3323 V are an excellent example and also come with an extra volume control switch situated on the lead. This extra volume control makes it possible to hear some of the softest voices. But there is a danger. Do not keep these phones on maximum volume unless you know the part of the tape you are examining. When your own voice starts to speak again on the tape you could end up with at best a nasty surprise, at worst burst eardrums. Work out the gaps between your cues either with a watch or with the tape machine's counter, if it's got one; and turn the volume down before your voice is heard again. If you prefer, you can record the piece of tape you want to examine onto another cassette, eliminating your voice entirely. That way you can safely use these types of headphones without any bother.

Tapes
Use only new tapes or cassettes: this will

eliminate any suggestion of an extraneous voice being due to a previous recording.

Don't skimp on the quality of the tapes or cassettes. Buy the best – which need not be the most expensive.

How to Proceed

Plug your external microphone into the cassette recorder and place it as far away from the machine as you can. Place a cushion over the tape machine if you can, to dampen the noise of the motor.

Place an unused tape or cassette in your machine, and start recording at maximum recording level.* Speak softly and stay as far as you like from the microphone, so that when you play back at full volume you don't deafen yourself. Give the voices ample time to reply. A minute or more is fine. Raudive recommends that each recording session lasts no more than a quarter of an hour or so. This is not because the owners of the voices lack staying power, but because of the monumental task involved in listening-in afterwards.

What to say

Better results are obtained if you ask specific questions or make specific comments than if you make a general invitation to "anyone out there" to leave a message on the tape. Don't worry if the

---

* I once recorded at a lower recording level by mistake. The result was that I could hardly hear my questions; but the recording level seemed to make no difference whatever to the audibility of the Raudive voices!

question you want to ask might sound silly: you are exploring unknown territory, and unusual questions can often reveal interesting and valuable information. I had heard a psychic medium on the radio claim to "see" the spirits of pet dogs. I asked my late wife during a recording session if she had had a reunion with the three cats we had once owned. When I played the tape back, there was a "yes" waiting for me. The inference from this is that some – if not all – animals have spiritual bodies. A "silly" question had produced possible confirmation of an important notion.

You can call up any person you like. Whether they reply or not is another matter. You are on safe ground if you stick to deceased friends and relatives. More adventurous souls might try to contact the famous. I don't recommend you do this unless you have a specific serious reason. Sometimes someone will come through who you have not asked to speak to. This means he wants to talk to you: communication can thus be maintained in the future.

The best way to *communicate* is to keep things simple. If possible, try to ask a question that can be answered with yes or no. The supersceptics' best shot at a rational explanation for the electronic voice phenomenon relies on the stray broadcast theory. This explanation occurred to me, as it occurred to the phenomenon's pioneers, Jürgenson and Raudive. The more questions that are answered with "yes" or "no", the further this incorrect explanation is left behind. If you are looking for a particular piece of information, tell the person you are contacting that you are going to read out a list of possible answers and to say yes after the correct one.

Listening~in

The listening-in process can be tedious while at the same time containing all the excitement of unwrapping a gift.

If you have tone controls on your equipment, you can switch off the bass. It has little – if anything – to contribute voicewise, and you may find the bass rumble offputting. Some of the treble hiss can be a nuisance, too. You may wish to reduce this hiss slightly. If your equipment has a graphic equaliser, you can minimise anything below 1Khz. Any other settings largely depend on how many slide controls you have. You will thus have to move them about by trial and error. You may wish to reduce the hiss above 10KHz.

Listening-in can, of course, take place immediately, next day, next week. You should play back at maximum volume or maximum tolerable volume. Don't just listen to the long gaps you left for the voices to reply in; listen also to the parts of the tape where you spoke. Sometimes a voice will come through in the gaps between words; sometimes a word spoken by a voice will coincide with a word spoken by you.

When you first begin to experiment, your sense of hearing will be undeveloped: you will only be able to hear grade A voices. As time goes on, your hearing will get used to listening for voices, and you will hear voices that you hitherto missed. Raudive says that three months is a typical time for an ear to become fully developed for listening-in to the electronic voice phenomenon.

But if you are a musician or a wireless operator you may learn to hear faster; you might even be lucky enough to hear grade B voices right from the start.

Sometimes most of the voices will be so soft that you can make out a background chatter without being able to make sense of what is being said. Most of this you will probably never be able to decipher. You may hear some chatter that is louder than the rest. Home in on this part of the tape and play it as many times as you like. You are recommended to write out what you hear phonetically. Once you have done this you can try to make sense of it. What you hear will probably be in one language, but be prepared for a foreign word to be slipped in here and there.

In Company
Although I recommend you to start out your researches alone, there is no reason why you shouldn't share your discoveries with others. Just bear in mind that the electronic voice phenomenon is not a show.

I would recommend that you choose who you pass on the information to carefully. People's reactions can vary. A lot of people will think you are mad – especially since hearing voices is a classic symptom of schizophrenia. Some people are ignorant sceptics who will regard an unexplained phenomenon as an intrusion into their neat little worlds. Others might have a distorted religious view and may regard contact with the dead as sinful.

If you want to hold a communal recording session, keep the numbers small: two, three or four people are ideal. Keep the amount of alcohol consumed to minimum or zero levels. Only invite good-natured people, and never invite anyone you know to be involved in satanic or sinister cults. Invite sceptics by all means. But the sceptic who will revise his theories in the face of new evidence will have most to benefit from these sessions. If one of your guests ruins the sessions by making wisecracks while the tape recorder is on, terminate the sessions as politely as possible and spend the rest of the evening playing bridge or Scrabble etc.

Invite your guests to ask whatever questions they wish. Let them contact dead friends or relatives. Play the tape back and listen for any grade A voices. If any are received, let people listen to the tape one at a time. If a grade A voice is good enough, you can play it to all on a loudspeaker. Grade B voices will have to be deciphered later and played to your friends when next you meet, or copied and given to them.

Is It Safe?

Some religious people – some of them clergymen – will tell you that you shouldn't be trying to contact the dead and that it's dangerous.

Should we be contacting the dead? Let's invert the question: are the dead allowed to contact us? They obviously seem to be. If it is in order for them to communicate with us, it must be in order for us to communicate with them.

Regarding danger. To the best of my knowledge nothing has happened either to Friedrich Jürgenson or to Konstantin Raudive, or to anyone else associated with the electronic voice phenomenon. To date, nothing has happened to me.

There is a hint from some of Konstantin Raudive's transcripts that on the other side access to the electronic voice phenomenon is restricted. "Customs" and "passports" are mentioned. This would tend to reinforce the notion that experimenting with the electronic voice phenomenon is perfectly safe.

As we shall see later, the messages are made with some kind of electromagnetic beam. This probably means that machinery is involved on the other side.

If there is any danger, it might come if someone tries to contact an entity who has been known to be wicked in his lifetime. This might attract a nasty presence. But I have never tried to do this, and I don't recommend it.

The more one learns about the whereabouts of the dead, (see Appendix B) the more one realises why experimenting with the electronic voice phenomenon is safe. It appears that you are not attracting entities that are not already there.

Who are we in touch with?
Believers in the supernatural can be as critical of the electronic voice phenomenon as any supersceptic; but their criticisms tend to be warnings that the entities producing the voices are mischievous or malevolent spirits – elementals. There is a possibility that elementals might be responsible for some impersonations. I honestly doubt this. Some voices have come onto tape and I have been able to identify the owner not by what he said but by the way he said it.

There are transcripts given in Raudive's *Breakthrough*, where Raudive stays up till all hours in his studio collecting voices. When he plays the tapes back and deciphers the voices, he finds them telling him it is late and he should get some sleep.

Would mischievous or malevolent spirits tell him that?

If it is the purpose of wicked entities to use the electronic voice phenomenon to drive people away from God and from goodness, then they have failed miserably!

Therefore, the best way we can treat the entities that produce the voices is the same way we would treat the clergy: we assume they are benign, while bearing in mind the possibility that they are not.

Further Experimentation

You needn't stay with the experiments outlined in this book. Further work on the electronic voice phenomenon is welcomed.

As well as the microphone method, both Raudive and Jürgenson managed to set up communication by radio. To do this, you really need to ask for help from the other side. Raudive and Jürgenson favoured the medium wave, but this is extremely crowded. Voices are supposed to be heard throughout the radio spectrum; so you may have success on, say, FM.

Raudive had success in recording with a diode, a device similar to the cat's whisker on an old crystal radio set, simple to construct for those versed in electronics. His friend, Theodor Rudolph, an electronics engineer, built a promising device which he called a goniometer circuit, based on crossed horizontal and vertical ferrite rods mounted on a magnet.

If you are at all electronically minded, you might want to try various devices based around small aerials (larger ones will just pick up radio broadcasts) and ferrite rods, to see if reception can be improved.

It might be worthwhile experimenting at improving reception with microphones. Raudive tried wedging a piece of wire in his microphone to act as an aerial, but it didn't seem to make much difference. Working on the assumption that the messages arrive on tape by electromagnetic beam, I placed some reflective material at beneficial angles around the microphone. Reception wasn't improved; nor was it harmed.

For those not electronically minded, there are still many questions that can be asked. Another thing you might wish to try is this: instead of asking a question by speaking onto tape, try thinking your question. See if you still get answers. My experiments have so far failed; you may have better success.

There is no limit to the things you can try, the questions you can ask.

Good hunting.

Behave Like a Scientist

Many of those on the scientific fringes have little

or no scientific training. Some even hold orthodox scientists in contempt, thinking they're really stupid.

They're not.

Scientists aren't eggheads with mussed hair and bow ties who sit doing sums all day – although a surprising number do answer to this description! Everything in science is measured, noted catalogued, filed.

Don't just make tape recordings. Keep a "laboratory notebook". Note down times, dates and contents of youir experiments. You can use your notebook to make transcripts of what the voices say to you. Before you begin asking questions to the entities from the world beyond, announce the date and the time of the experiment. If you like, number the experiment, and announce the number on tape, writing it down in your notebook.

That way, if your experiments are ever subjected to scientific scrutiny, you will have conducted your experiments correctly, and are thus more likely to be taken seriously.

Rational Explanations of the Phenomenon

It is not easy to find an explanation that avoids life after death, but there have been tries.

The most notable attempt came from David Ellis, a Trinity College, Cambridge, research student who had obtained a Perrott Warwick Studentship in order to study the electronic voice phenomenon. His findings were published in *The Journal of the Society for Psychical Research* in

1975. In essence, Ellis says that the electronic voice phenomenon is due to stray radio broadcasts and the imaginations of the experimenters.

Ellis's findings were trumpeted, along with findings of his own, by Stanley Gooch in his book, *The Paranormal*. Gooch's findings are that occasionally taxi firms come through on modern hi fi equipment, and cites one case where the soundtrack of a film being shown at a cinema two hundred metres down the road came through on his friend's music centre. He finishes his section on the electronic voice phenomenon by summing it up in one word: rubbish. However, Mr. Gooch is no friend of the atheist or the sceptic: in the very same book, Mr. Gooch, who claims to have psychic powers, says that whereas the electronic voice phenomenon doesn't work, tarot cards and the I Ching do. We must, however, respect Mr. Gooch's right to criticise and it behoves us to look at his criticisms carefully, even though I, too, can sum them up in a single word: inadequate.

The Ellis/Gooch model does contain a lot of truth and underlines one or two problems with the electronic voice phenomenon. The first is the interpretation of what the voices say. There was a now legendary television advertisement for a brand of cassette tape. It used the lyrics of the reggae classic by Desmond Dekker and the Aces: *The Israelites:*

> *I get up in the morning,*
> *Slaving for bread, sir,*
> *So that every mouth can be fed.*
> *Oo~ooh, the Israelites.*

The advertisement shows a Rastafarian holding up boards on which is written what he hears as a consequence of not using the advertiser's brand of cassette. The second line becomes "slaving for breakfast". The fourth line becomes "oo-ooh, me ears are alight". I was at school when *The Israelites* was topping the charts. I had a classmate who sang it once in a while; and I do remember him singing "slaving for breakfast".

It all goes to show that the voices on the tape could indeed be misinterpreted, and in many cases they are. The faintness of many of the voices and the speed at which they speak (about twice the speed of normal speech) only exacerbate the problem. There are some voices I have received where I have several possible interpretations of what the voice might have said; and I can't decide which interpretation is the most likely, let alone which one is correct. The confusion is often clarified when the experimenter uses context as a guide to interpretation.

Matters are further complicated when a polyglot like Dr. Raudive is involved. Dr. Raudive will look at several languages when interpreting his messages. This is a curious feature of the voices, a feature first noticed by Jürgenson. The feature is typified by the title of my SF novelette, *Do Det Ike*. The title comes from a Raudive voice the story's protagonist receives on a tape recorder. The three words are *do* (English), *det* (Danish for "it"), *ike* (based on *ikke*, the Danish word for "not"). You put the whole message together and you get "don't do it." The messages received by Jürgenson and Raudive are mainly in Swedish and Latvian respectively. But their messages are peppered with neologisms, and words pinched from French, German, English, Spanish, Latin and any other European language you care to think of. Others, particularly Peter Bander, who wrote the preface to *Breakthrough*, have only ever received voices in one language. I have only received voices either in Standard English or Scottish English (contactor and contactee are both Scots.) I am, however, willing to accept that the entities who produce the voices are limited by rhythmn and – probably – voice pattern, and have to use words wherever they can find them.

Bander places the polyglottal nature of the voices on Raudive himself. The same would also apply to Jürgenson – another polyglot. But Peter Bander is a polyglot, too. So am I.

The difference therefore must be the main language we are addressed in. Raudive's main language is Latvian. Latvian is one of three Baltoslav languages – the others being Lithuanian and Old Prussian. It is a relatively pure language, lightly contaminated by Latvia's German and Russian neighbours. Jürgenson's Swedish is a descendant of Old Norse, but with the simplified grammar shared by Norwegian, Danish and English. It is even less contaminated than Latvian. English, however, was originally the language of the Angles. Added to Anglish, are words of Danish origin introduced when Britain was invaded and settled by the Vikings. French words were added after the Norman Conquest. Classical scholars added words of Latin and Greek origin later. The British Empire has added words of non European origin; and more words from Australia, South Africa and North America are constantly being added. The complete English vocabulary consists of something like half a million words. Other languages – including Swedish and Latvian – have vocabularies only a fraction of this size. Small wonder Raudive's voices have to use Old Latvian, Latgalian dialect and foreign languages to fit their rhythmns. But the English language is so rich, a word that will fit can always be found.

The other problem that Ellis and Gooch bring up is stray broadcasts breaking onto the recording tape. This situation can happen. Radio broadcasts have also been known to come through on other electric appliances like electric kettles; and, in one celebrated American case, on dental bridgework. You can reduce – though not eliminate – this possibility from happening by using a tape recorder that hasn't got a radio: there will be no aerial or ferrite rod to pick up stray broadcasts. But even if you use a radio/cassette player to record voices from the next world rogue radio broadcasts are rare.

Tests were carried out in Pye Studios in London during the early 1970s. Precautions were taken to filter out stray broadcasts. In the space of 27 minutes some 200 voices were received, making converts of the two sceptical Pye sound engineers who supervised the experiments.

But you can demolish the stray broadcast argument yourself without special equipment. Turn your radio on and, turning the tuning knob, run it up and down the dial. It doesn't matter if you are set in FM, AM or whatever. You will notice that a large percentage of broadcasts – perhaps the majority of them – consist of music. Yet music never comes through – not when you are recording by microphone. That means that if radio is interfering with the tape recorders, we can only restrict ourselves to the non broadcast bands: taxi firms, police, citizen's band etc. Raudive was a Latvian. His voices spoke in Latvian in Sweden, Germany, U.S.A. – any country he recorded in.

This is what you can do to disprove the stray broadcast theory to yourself, if not to others. Ask as many questions as possible that can be answered with just a yes or a no. In English we have a relatively complicated word for the affirmative: yes. To get a yes, you need a palatalisation, followed by a hard e, followed by a hiss. You can't really mistake the word yes for anything else; and you can't really mistake anything else for the word yes. Time after time, questions you ask will be answered with this word. Then you will have no possible doubt that you and the owners of the voices are *communicating.*

Another way the stray broadcast theory falls is the fact that some of the voices received come in the form of whispers. Another piece of evidence occurred during one of my questions to the world beyond. The question I was asking included the words, "...my forthcoming book..." (The one you are reading now!) When I played the tape back, the voice of one of my deceased relatives intruded in a tone of joking mockery: "Your forthcoming book!"

There is, though, a genuine problem for any outsider who wants to sit in on research into the electronic voice phenomenon. I have mentioned it in the section on listening-in. Because the sense of hearing has to be fully developed before grade B and grade C voices can be heard properly, there is a definite aural skills gap for the new observer. By the time he has developed his sense of hearing he is sceptical no more!

Other rational explanations for the electronic voice phenomenon become somewhat irrational. According to one, the subconscious uses psychokinesis to place the voices on tape. Let us say, for argument's sake, that this were possible. Most experimenters wouldn't know how a voice is actually *put* onto magnetic tape. Not even that great psychological dumping ground, the subconscious, can do the unknown.

A rational explanation has been found for the near death experience, largely because most of the evidence is verbal. With the electronic voice phenomenon, there is concrete evidence with a simple experiment that can be repeated by anybody.

How the Electronic Voice Phenomenon Compares to the Near Death Experience

Is the world glimpsed by the near death experience the same as the one described by the voices that manifest themselves on tape?

The World of the Near Death Experience

What is felt by so many of the near death experiencers is the powerful feeling of love. So strong is this feeling that many experiencers simply don't want return to their earthly bodies.

There is a suggestion that what happens to the

experiencer from the moment he leaves his earthly body until his return is not exactly the next dimension. There is often a boundary, sometimes a fence, sometimes a river. The experiencer is told that once that boundary is crossed he can never return to his earthly body. For that reason, in all but a few cases, the information the experiencer comes back with is scant. Often the experiencer complains that language is simply inadequate to describe the things he has sensed.

This is quite understandable. Some say they saw colours they had never seen before. How would you describe, say, blue to someone who had never seen it?

But some information does slip through about life in the next dimension. Education is a fundamental occupation of the inhabitants of the next world. A "university" exists where people's life experiences are pooled with other knowledge.

There is a feeling that *everything* in the Universe – or maybe we should now call it Multiverse – is interconnected. This feeling of interconnectedness overpowers many near death experiencers and completely changes the way they view the world and spend the rest of their lives.

The notion of guardian angels or spirit helpers gets support from near death experiencers. But there is no specific angel set the task of looking after you throughout your life. There are at least two – maybe more – and personnel seem interchangeable.

There is one serious sin: homicide – whether it be your own life or someone else's.

This brings us to the subject of Hell, which I

will deal with in more detail later. About 0.3% of accounts from near death experiencers are negative ones, often involving demons, descents to hell, fire and lost souls begging for water.

Time and again the experiencer returns with the news that love is by far the most important thing in life, with knowledge in second place.

The Electronic Voice Phenomenon's Hereafter.
Here the information is confused and often contradictory. This is hardly surprising seeing that communication from the world beyond is both curt and difficult. The problem is not so much what information the voices give us but what questions to ask.

Voices say there are difficulties in the world beyond, although they are fine. One of Jürgenson's guests once remarked that everybody was happy and carefree in the hereafter. A voice answered: "Nonsense!"

I mentioned above that near death experiencers have seen people in hell asking for water. Some enigmatic voices have been received by Raudive, asking for water. They have also asked for bread, cigarettes, cognac etc.

Some voices mention wars and armies. I will deal with this later.

Other voices say that Hitler, a genocide and a suicide, is in the world beyond. Voices claiming to be Hitler and other members of the German National Socialist Party have been received, too.

Surely this can't be the same dimension full of love experienced by those who have died and have been resuscitated.

Or can it?

Reconciling the Two

One significant question that was asked by Raudive was that this life is just one of many lives that we lead. His answer told him that he was correct.

I will summarise the information we have, brought back by near death experiencers. When we die, we leave our earthly bodies, become aware of our spiritual body and meet the spiritual bodies of others whom we knew in our earthly lifetimes. We then travel along a tunnel to a place of light and love, and there meet a being of light who reviews our earthly life. The being of light then tells us that if we cross a certain border we can never return to our earthly bodies.

The earthly body, the spiritual body, the being of light: three types of entity.

The earth, the place at the end of the tunnel, the place across the border: three different realms.

It is significant also that voices received on tape come from those dead within the past hundred years or so. Hitler has left his voice on tape. Churchill has. Tolstoi has. Julius Caesar has not, nor Elijah, nor Tutenkhamen. Why not? Have they been reincarnated? Or have they gone to other – to higher – planes of existence?

Therefore, our life on Earth is the first – or one of the first – planes of existence. When we die, a being of light often asks: "Have you learned to love?" Well, have we? We are then sent "over the border" to a spiritual plane, where we must prepare for the next stage of existence, which may be in the realm of the beings of light.

Learning to love is a difficult thing, as I will show you later. Small wonder many of the voices that come through on Raudive's tapes complain of hardship.

Wisdom from the World Beyond

The near death experiencers all bring back the same message about the two most important things in this life: love and knowledge.

Naturally, I put this to the entities on the other side during one of my sessions with the tape recorder. I received the following answer in a grade A voice:

"Thus."

Love
This has long been known as one of life's essentials, since the time of Christ, and probably long before that.

It is the most important thing in the world. It is easy and difficult at the same time. Most of us know love through our marriages, our families. Of course, not every family is awash with love. Some families are a veritable hell on Earth.

No man is an island, and love must be seen in context with the rest of humanity. So, now knowing that love is the most important thing, we set out in the morning to take our loyal and loving dog for a walk. On the way, we meet a neighbour. We bid him a cheery "Good Morning!" and in reply all we get is a scowl.

We go to work with a sublime smile, only to find the boss saying to us: "What the hell are

you grinning at?"
And how many times have we gone out of our way to help people only to be met with ingratitude and a metaphorical kick in the teeth?

Love would be much easier without other people. But then we'd have no one to love!

Knowledge

This will come as a surpise to many people, since many of those who possess it all too often have to suffer for it.

Think of the put-down lines: "too clever by half", "know-all", "curiosity killed the cat". There are lots more. Perhaps the most often used is "a little knowledge is a dangerous thing". This is a misquote from Alexander Pope's *Essay on Criticism*, and is often used by those who recommend that you should be as ignorant as they. Pope was giving instruction to would-be literary critics. The whole verse quoted shows that he was not telling us to stay ignorant:

A little learning is a dang'rous thing;
Drink deep, or taste not the Pierian spring:
There shallow draughts intoxicate the brain,
And drinking largely sobers us again.

This philosophy is known worldwide. It is no accident, for example, that in Japanese martial arts, the beginner wears a white belt. He then works his way through an assortment of colours and many grades of black belt. When he knows everything - or nearly everything - he then has the right to wear the highest possible colour of belt: a white belt.

The acquisition of knowledge, like the acquisition of love, comes naturally to some people. Others have been through an education system, and their education stopped the day they left school or university. Others have rejected the acquisition of knowledge from the very beginning.

The current World Chess Champion, Garry Kasparov, was a chess prodigy in his youth. He was thus allowed to travel abroad to play in foreign chess tournaments – something of a rare privilege in the Soviet Union. When he returned to Azerbaijan, he was eager to tell his friends and acquaintances about the wonderful things he had seen in foreign lands. In his autobiography, *Child of Change*, he states he was dismayed to find that most people didn't want to listen to him.

One thing I am certain of, so far as the acquisition of knowledge is concerned: we must not treat our acquired knowledge like a pinchpenny treats money. It must be shared so that others can use it.

For that reason, I give below some of the most important pieces of information I have received from the world beyond via the tape recorder.

Where are They?
Q. Are you in another dimension?
A. Yes.

No really hard evidence of parallel universes existed until now. The subject is dealt with in more detail in Appendix B. There are some enigmatic messages about the dead being still among us contained in Raudive's transcripts. Here we have have probable clarification.

Psychic Mediums
Before the death of my wife, I had assumed psychic mediums were at best imaginative and at worst fraudulent. However, the following messages on the tape endorse psychic mediumship.

Q. There are spiritualist mediums who claim to be able to contact the world beyond. Are there such people, or do they suffer from a fevered imagination?
A. It's possible.

Q. N---, would you prefer that in order to contact you I went to a good psychic medium?
A. Yes.

Although these answers allow us to give psychic mediums some credence, it does not tell us how to recognise a good medium from one whose psychic powers are poorly developed or an outright fake.

Hell
I spent a great deal of time and effort with the tapes on this subject. This is mainly because I didn't believe in hell when I was practising Roman Catholicism in my youth.
One episode of the celebrated SF television series *Dr Who* has the following situation.
The series's villain, The Master (illustriously played by the late Roger Delgado), has, due to the failure of his own universe-conquering machinations, incurred the wrath of an all-powerful entity. Dr. Who (Jon Pertwee) is given

the choice of sentencing The Master to eternal torment or letting him go free. "Let him go", says the Doctor. The entity reluctantly frees The Master so that he can cause more mayhem in future episodes. Afterwards, Dr. Who's assistant Jo (Katy Manning) asks why.
Dr. Would you sentence anyone to eternal torment - even The Master?
Jo. No.
 Neither would I.

 A Christian would argue that since Christ in the gospels intimates that God has unlimited capacity to forgive, then there can't be a hell.
 It would seem that this is not so.
 I asked the following question on tape, receiving answers while I was speaking. The answers are given in the brackets.

Q. If there is a hell, are people there sent eternally [*Yes.*] as the churches teach [*No*]...

 This is an interesting answer. There is, according to the voice, eternal damnation. But what is the nature of Hell? If it is not the eternal torment promised by the churches, there could then be two possibilities.
 The person is sent to a lower plane where he may have some form of happiness, but is forever cut off from the full glory that is the reward of everyone else.
 The alternative is finely illustrated by an old Oriental parable.
 A great man died. As a reward for his life's great deeds he was given the choice of going to Heaven or to Hell after being allowed a visit to

both places. First the man visited Hell. There he saw a huge table laden with the finest food he had ever seen. But everyone sitting at the table was miserable. "Why?" the man asked them. One of them answered: "It's the rule here that we must eat with chopsticks that are two metres long. We thus can't get the food into our mouths, so we can't eat and enjoy the food, and we go hungry." The man then went to Heaven. But there was no difference: the table was lavishly set, and each person has a pair of two metre chopsticks. Yet everyone was happy. "What's the difference between Heaven and Hell?" the man asked. "There isn't any," someone answered; "except here we feed each other."

This must be partly true: it is largely people's attitude that makes the difference between Heaven and Hell.

However, the voices don't seem to agree with either of these models.

Q. Is hell a place of eternal torment?
A. Yes.

This is sad news for the merciful among us. Of course, this torment can take many forms, including a feeling of eternal perdition.

My old schoolteacher – the same one who said that for every virtue there is a vice – brought his Mancunian philosophy to bear on the subject of Hell. He said: I reckon there are only about six people in Hell: people are either not bad enough to go there, or else they're mad and can't be held responsible for their actions.

My teacher may have underestimated the

population of Hell; but, among near death experiencers, negative experiences, including descents in a downward direction, demons and even a glimpse of Satan himself, account for only about 0.3% of near death experiences. If we apply this percentage to the British population, somewhere in the region of 100,000 to 180,000 of the people alive in this country today are hellbound. I personally think that 0.3% is on the high side, especially since it includes one account of a man who was sent down to hell by mistake and was turned away at the gates! Because of the relatively small numbers involved in the research, this one case would have a significant effect on the percentage. Another thing that would make the hell percentage higher than it should be is the fact that among those more likely to have near death experiences are autodestroyers like drug abusers and attempted suicides. The negative near death experience acts as a stiff warning: change your ways or.... They invariably change their ways. Bearing this in mind, the numbers of people in this country who are hellbound will be a good deal less.

I asked the tape recorder one last question on the subject of Hell.

Q. In order to get to Hell, do you really have to blot your copybook?
A. Yes.

99.997% of us can breathe a sigh of relief!

War
Some of the messages received by Raudive had

me puzzled. Wars were mentioned. A woman who had passed on was asked for. The experimenter was told that the woman concerned was unavailable because she was in the army.

I asked about this subject on the tape. What was going on over there? What was all this talk about armies and wars? Do they have wars in the world beyond?

In reply I received a loud, emphatic whisper: "No war!"

Setting Up Contact
As I have already reported, it took three months for Raudive to set up contact. I received my voice after a week. I asked:

Q. Am I correct in thinking that it takes time to set up contact?
A. Yes.

God
My 11 year old son asked this of his dead mother.

Q. Is there a God.
A. Yes.

Time!?
Some of the voices tell Raudive that there is no time where they are. This is something echoed by those who have come back from a near death experience. Certainly a whole life has been shown to them while they have been "dead" for more than about a minute.

By applying my own logic to this, I came up

with an unusual question.

Q. If there is no time where you are, then it should be possible for me to communicate with myself. Am I right?
A. [Total silence]

I had bamboozled even the inhabitants of the world beyond!

**The Near Death Experience,
the Electronic Voice Phenomenon and Religion**
The near death experiencer brings back the clear message that religious denomination doesn't matter. The life you have lived is judged on its merits. Most sensible people knew that anyway.

The religious teachings of what is in store for us after death varies from denomination to denomination. The truth is that most religions simply don't know what is in store for us after death: they base their teachings largely on scripture, some of which might indeed be based on near death experiences.

Raudive, himself a practising Catholic, reached the conclusion that the world he was contacting resembled the Catholic Purgatory. But even this can only be a compromise with doctrine. From the first moment of my own Catholic education we were taught that those in Purgatory were to be pitied. Collections were held for the "Holy Souls", the money going towards the cost of the masses celebrated on their behalf. Officially the Catholic Church is divided into three parts: the

Church Militant (those on Earth), the Church Suffering (those in Purgatory) and the Church Triumphant (those in Heaven). But, as we have seen via the near death experience and the electronic voice phenomenon, those who have gone onto the next dimension , although they might be suffering, they are not suffering nearly so much as those in the Church Militant.

As I have said earlier, the near death experience has allowed humanity a glimpse of three entities: earthly bodies, spiritual bodies and beings of light. An orthodox Christian might interpret these three stages of existence as inhabitants of Earth, Purgatory and Heaven respectively. But who said the being of light was in Heaven? I would speculate that the being of light is just another stage – that there are other lives beyond that one. Perhaps the staging process goes on for ever.

Those of a religious persuasion, having been through a near death experience, sometimes give up their religion because what they have seen doesn't equate with what their religion teaches.

Some clergymen have had near death experiences. One had preached fire and brimstone from his pulpit until he went through a life review with a being of light. When he returned to his pulpit his tone was softer; instead of preaching fire and eternal damnation, he preached love.

In the light of the information we have, we can see that many of the silly things taught and demanded by religion become rather insignificant. We live not just on Earth, not just in a vast and possibly infinite universe even; but in a multiverse. Seen in this context it is easy to see that you are not going to be damned for ever if you work on the Sabbath, eat pork, use artificial birth control, miss mass, or show your face and limbs in public. There is only one set of guidelines you need follow: how best to love your fellow man.

Therefore practise a religion if you want, disobey its rules if your conscience demands it; or stay away from the churches and live your own life by your own rules. It really doesn't matter which choice you make.

Reincarnation
This can't be ignored: so many people believe in it, and there seems to be some evidence pointing in its direction.

The notion of reincarnation is worldwide, but is especially common in the Far East. Many believe that we come back not only as people, but as insects and animals, too.

The most publicised evidence in Britain of reincarnation is the many hypnotic regressions performed by Fred Keating among others.

In these cases, the hypnotist instructs his hypnotised subject to go back to a time before he was born. The subject might then recall a character from a past century.

The beliefs of some people who are into reincarnation can provide some amusement for the sceptic. There are some people who believe that one of their pet animals is a reincarnation of a dead relative. Some reincarnation believers think that homosexuality is caused by having been someone of the opposite sex in a past life. If we follow this argument to its logical conclusion, bestiality is caused by someone having been an animal in a past life; paedophilia is caused by someone in a past life dying while still a child. I'm afraid I can't think of an explanation for bisexuality.

The biggest laughs of all must be reserved for those who think they were someone famous in a past life. More than one person has said they were Mary Queen of Scots in a past life, and cite as evidence a birthmark on their necks - the remnant of her beheading. Another popular decapitated queen is Anne Bullen.* Julius Caesar is another popular past life.

Derision aside, there have been a few cases of people who have regressed and have apparently confounded historians with their detail which has sometimes defied historians' beliefs and was later found to be correct. (This is not so convincing as it sounds: historians disagree among themselves, are specialised in different fields etc; some historians have more up-to-date information than others. (No pun intended!) There are many explanations for this apparent evidence:

a) the regression is evidence of reincarnation;

b) the regression is concocted in the imagination of the subject and agrees with the historical evidence by coincidence;

---

* Also known as Anne Boleyn.

c) the regression is a hoax;

d) the hypnotised subject is recalling something he has seen, heard or read;

e) the hypnotised subject is recalling a genetic memory;

f) the hypnotised subject is recalling part of a collective human subconscious.

Working on the information brought back by near death experiencers, we might add:

g) contact has been made not with a hypnotised subject, but with his spirit helpers (guardian angels).

g) does fit the evidence. The hypnotiser usually tells the subject that he must only narrate events that have actually happened to him. If a person is a multiplicity of selves, as suggested by the writer Colin Wilson, then the events that have happened to a spirit helper could be construed as having happened to the subject.

As spirit helpers are supposed to be interchangeable, g) might explain why there are so many Mary Queen of Scots about. But then so does b)!

It is not, however, inconceivable that some reincarnation does take place. Consider a child who lives until he is four years old and then dies. Is he ready to start the next life? Or is he sent out again in another body to live a complete life?

I brought up the subject on the tape recorder. Firstly I announced the subject of the question: "Reincarnation;" then I paused while I thought about the wording of the question. When I played the tape back, during the pause, a male voice said: "Rubbish!"

Repercussions
Dostoyevski in the Grand Inquisitor chapter of *The Brothers Karamazov* stated that humankind could never be certain of God and the afterlife, because that would take away his freedom - his free will. "Didst thou forget that man prefers peace, and even death, to freedom of choice in the knowledge of good and evil?" What Dostoyevski here means is that if humankind *knows* there is life after death, that there is a life review where his actions are examined, all he has to do is follow the rules of God and he will get to Heaven. We have some guidelines brought back by near death experiencers and heard on the tape recorder. All we have to do is follow these simple guidelines and we are saved?

It's not as simple as that. Dostoyevski,* one of the greatest authors of all time - assuming he himself held the views aired in *The Brothers Karamazov* - chooses a philosophy that falls short. To be fair, other philosophers have made the same speculation, and Dostoyevski lived in a time when thanatology was practically non

---
* Voices claiming to be Dostoyevski appeared on tape to Raudive and are transcribed in *Breakthrough.*

existent. Life after death had not been proved, and it looked certain that it would never be proved. Indeed it wasn't proved until the publication of Jürgenson's *Rosterna från Rymden* in 1964.

"Give bread," says Dostoyevski, "and man will worship you, for nothing is more certain than bread." The bread in question is the certainty of an afterlife. Dostoyevski reasoned that once they knew where their bread was coming from, everyone would worship in that direction. The truth of the matter is that certain knowledge of an afterlife just throws up a new set of problems.

Suddenly the whole of life is seen in the context of a glimpse of the afterlife. We know that killing is the most serious sin of all. But how do we interpret this? What about a kill-or-be-killed situation? Abortion? Mercy killing – of human beings or horses? Killing for food? Stamping on a cockroach on the kitchen floor? Leaving out rat poison? And what about wishing yourself dead, and dying of what the sentimentalists call a broken heart?

To give an example of the new problems involved, let us focus on one topical example: the reintroduction of the death penalty for murder. How would the information we have from the world beyond affect our reasoning?

The classic argument against the death penalty is that there may be a miscarriage of justice. Those who advocate the death penalty might argue that by hanging someone who is innocent is actually doing that person a favour by sending him to the promised land. The counter argument is that the murder is committed in this plane, and the problem of what to do with the murderer must therefore be dealt with in this plane. The murderer must be given time here to face up to the consequences of what he has done. Even if he spends the rest of his life in a prison, his time can be used usefully, perhaps even to atone for what he has done. There are of course many other arguments concerning the death penalty, and the miscarriage of justice argument will make sure that capital punishment is no longer used in Britain.

There was a case recently where, during a murder trial, three jurors used a ouija board to try to contact the murder victim. They asked her if the defendant had killed her. When the ouija board had spelled out a yes, whether by spiritual means or otherwise, those jurors decided to find the defendant guilty. Fortunately, a fourth juror, more level headed than the other three, reported the incident to the judge, who rightly ordered a retrial, where the defendant was found guilty anyway.

This book does not examine the pros and cons of ouija boards, planchettes and the like. The murder trial incident more than anything else shows that often the addition of the afterlife into this world's affairs is both a complication and an intrusion. The current state of affairs is that the next world never counts in the solution of problems of this world. Long may it remain so. But I know from my own experience that the future of all of us after death must affect everything that happens here.

This leads us inevitably to the problem of

what we are going to do with the rest of our lives. The answer would appear to be that we shouldn't do much more than we are doing at the moment – that the greater majority of us don't really need to be "saved".

The near death experiencers bring back the news that religious denomination – or lack of it – doesn't really matter. But there are little things we can do to make this world a better place. It is on these that we are judged.

The review of our life at our deaths is a fair one. It is not like a court case. We are not judged on *what* we have done, but on our motivation or our foolishness. Therefore, if we send a business letter and quote the addressee's reference number correctly, we have done a good thing. If we quote an incorrect reference number which has a clerk at the other end searching for the correct file for two hours we are not taken to task...unless we quoted the incorrect number deliberately in order to create as much chaos as possible. If we simply made a mistake, we are not hellbound. If we are driving a car, forget to look before switching lanes and kill someone in the process, we would not be admonished after our death, no matter what misery we caused. If, however, we had been drinking alcohol before the accident, we would probably be made to experience the victim's family's pain and misery. If we had deliberately forced another vehicle off the road for a reason other than self defence, then that would be regarded as a very serious matter indeed.

Motivation is a difficult point. And here the atheist has a definite advantage over the theist; and is, ironically, probably closer to God than his God-fearing equivalent.

Many theists crawl to their clergy, crawl to their god, in the hope of salvation in the same way that the office creep crawls to the boss while looking for promotion. The office creep might get his promotion; the theistic creep might move on to the next plane. What neither of them will get is respect, either from their peers or from their bosses.

Many theists will do good deeds because they want to please their god. The atheist by definition cannot do anything for this reason. There are thus two other reasons: he does it for his own benefit or for the benefit of others.

When the life review with the being of light comes, if your motivation in doing a good deed was to gain you favour in the next life, this will show: since communication is entirely by thought, you can't hide anything.

This is not to say that religious motivation is always a bad thing. There are many missionaries alleviating human suffering in the third world simply out of religious conviction. Our prisons and mental hospitals would even more resemble human dustbins than they do without the many Quakers who have embraced these unpopular causes.

You might be better living a secular life, always bearing in mind the comfort and rights of your fellow humans. I doubt if you are required to do "great" things with your life. One man who has in modern times done more great things than just about anyone else is Thomas Alva Edison. The betterment of the human race might not have been his prime motive; but the effects of just the most famous of his inventions – the electric light – are there to behold... in almost every home in the developed world. But while Edison was engaged in inventing electric light, the phonograph, the motion picture etc., someone was emptying his dustbin, delivering his mail.

As those of us who live in the real world know already, lofty ambitions are for the very rich. For the rest of us there is the daily grind of making enough money to buy food, pay one's rent. This means, I am afraid, most of us will have to give up the idea of teaching English and mathematics in a remote African village, or genetically engineering a strain of wheat that will grow anywhere anytime and feed the starving masses in favour of feeding ourselves and our families.

I believe it is important to think for ourselves. There are so many theists who allow their religion to do the thinking for them. The religious package comes complete with a set of morals which you are advised – and in too many cases ordered – to follow.

There is nothing wrong with going to a clergyman for advice on, say, a domestic problem: the clergy, along with counsellors, agony aunts, lawyers, social workers etc, have experience of dealing with people's troubles, and can thus give people invaluable information and access to helpful organisations. But too often the theist goes to a clergyman not for advice but for a command. Whatever the clergyman says, the theist will follow even when that person's "nose" tells him to do something else.

For that reason, I should think it correct that

you should decide for yourself on moral matters. It is not impossible: atheists have been doing it for hundreds of years. Not to do so is to surrender your free will.

Moral Troubles

So now we know what is in store for us when we die everything is hunky dory. Right?

It should be, but for many it won't be.

The difference from traditional religious belief is that we no longer *believe*; we *know*. This leads to a problem that hasn't really been encountered since the Reformation.

Let us take a theist and make him, for argument's sake, a Catholic. One day he decides that he doesn't like the idea of the Blessed Trinity. He decides to give up Catholicism. He can adopt a religion that is more suitable for his tastes and beliefs: he can become a Mormon or a Lutheran or a Buddhist, or anything he likes. He can even turn his back on religion altogether. But, if he *knew* that there were three Gods in one, he might not like it, but there would be nothing he could do about it.

In my own religious days, I did not accept Hell. Since I have communicated with the other side, I have been forced to accept it as reality. I'm not happy about it, but there you are.

And this is the big problem.

What happens if you see something in the afterlife that you fundamentaly disagree with?

Does this mean that you will be sent to Hell yourself? Probably not. There will, no doubt, be good reasons why all these things are the way they are. The good reasons will be revealed to us in due course in the next life, if not in this one.

This means, of course, that the big question remains unanswered. We have a world, a universe, now a multiverse...just what is it all for?

O.K. It is now becoming clear that this world is some kind of proving ground? Why? To make mistakes that we can learn from for our next life.

We have just had a glimpse of what is in store for us. Some of us will accept this happily. Others will be horrified.

There are many atheists who have not actually given up belief in God. Instead they have rejected Him. This is the type of atheist who says: "If God is so good, why is there so much evil and suffering in the world?" It's a good question. Religion hasn't come up with a good enough answer as to why some people are born in perfect health, while others are born into broken bodies and have to live their entire lives often in intense pain; why some people can die quickly with little or no pain and others have to endure months of intense pain before leaving this life. Often used by the clergy is the quote from St. Paul: "Our ways are not the ways of the Lord." Dead right.

Another argument is that most of the problems on this Earth are caused by humans themselves. This is not entirely true, but it is certainly true that we have it within ourselves to make things a lot better than they are.

For instance, in Britain there are many suicides that can be directly attributed to the actions of of government policy. There are people who haven't worked for years, youngsters who have never worked in their lives apart from a stint on a youth work experience programme. Towns with a high unemployment rate also have a high suicide rate. Further suicides are said to have been caused by the high-handed action of the Child Support Agency, who have brought many fathers to the brink of financial ruin and then pushed them over the edge.

As we no longer take a universal but a multiversal view of things, we know that government policy have caused these poor folk not only misery on this side of death, but on the other side as well. Perhaps the beings of light will take the misery and mayhem caused by government policy into account when deciding what to do with these suicides.

Indeed the whole question of suicide is worrying. Near death experiencers bring back the message that on the other side suicide is regarded as a very serious misdemeanour because the suicide is throwing the gift of life back in God's face. People commit suicide for all kinds of reasons: mental illness, avoidance of capture, avoidance of torture, avoidance of pain, despair. In Japan, it is still part of the culture that a man dishonoured is expected to disembowel himself. For that reason, Japan has the world's highest suicide rate. But I have never, ever heard of anyone killing themselves because they wanted to throw the gift of life back in God's face!

There is thankfully an account of a mega near death experience from a wounded soldier during the Second World War. This soldier was taken on a tour of the afterlife by a being of light. Among the things the soldier saw were the places of learning, laboratories that were equipped for sciences that were well beyond the ken of a 1940s soldier. Among the other things he saw were suicides being told by beings of light about the misery they had caused their families. He also saw people that were so angry they were hitting each other with cudgels. Others in the same room were performing anger-motivated lewd sex acts on each other. Also in the room were beings of light begging them to stop – that it wasn't too late to save themselves from eternal damnation.

It seems that the afterlife is there for anyone who really wants it.

The Way Forward

What do we do now that we know there is a life after death, and we have some idea of what it contains?

Let me first state what I would not want to see.

I am not trying to start a religion. I would not want to see the knowledge in this book being used as the foundation of a faith with rules, clergy, hierarchy, dogma and bigotry – all the things that have conspired to prevent people from living their God-given lives to the full.

There is no need to try to ram newly-acquired knowledge down people's throats. Unlike Christian fundamentalist sects, we know that we needn't "save" other people: we know from both the near death experience and the electronic voice phenomenon that they are in all probability saved anyway.

Dostoyevski and other philosophers have speculated that the certain knowledge of an afterlife will change everything - will affect the way humanity thinks. I don't believe much will change. The priorities of the human race are still survival and the production of the next generation. Others will reject the knowledge and will continue to behave in an anti-social manner. There will be some who, knowing that beings of light on the other side have a high degree of tolerance, will take liberties "knowing" they will be forgiven in the end; perhaps they will.

There will certainly be resistance to us experimenting with the electronic voice phenomenon. Some psychics might warn that it is dangerous and circulate rumours about houses being invaded by evil spirits. Some theists will warn about contacting the devil by tape recorder. Rationalists will scoff. With what we now know, we can decide not to take their advice. The entities who contact us are learning to love and are acquiring knowledge. They are not evil. They couldn't be. The entities I have identified were good people while they were living here on Earth, so they are even better people now.

Some readers may have read this book and have decided to take the contents on trust without trying any of the experiments. I recommend you don't blindly believe anything in this book. Test the contents out to your satisfaction. There is no substitute for certainty. Certainty is your best armour against criticism and against the recent rise in the popularity of religious fundamentalism. Therefore ask the owners of Raudive voices whatever will convince you of life after death.

Hold conversations with your loved ones if you wish. It seems that they want to converse with you.

There is enough misery in the world without bereavement. If a son or daughter goes on a trip away from home a parent will be anxious until a letter, a post card or a telephone call is received from that offspring. That communication tells us that he or she has arrived safely and everything is fine.

We are sad when we lose someone close to us due to death. For some the loss is so devastating that they will kill themselves, or simply pine away. But, thanks to the electronic voice phenomenon, we have a message from our loved one to say that he or she has arrived in the next world safely and everything is fine. Like the worried parent, the difference the message from the world beyond makes is enormous. Suddenly, we can get on with the rest of our lives knowing that we will meet again in due course. We need worry about them no more, although they may still worry about us.

If you are involved in study, don't abandon your subject to devote all your time to looking beyond our horizon. There is still plenty about our Earth, our Universe, our own bodies that we still don't know. The near death experiencers tell us that everything is interconnected. Therefore no science is more important than another; so it doesn't matter if you are studying or researching cosmology, theology, languages or local history.

In Britain, over the past decade and a half, the political pendulum has swung away from cooperation and towards individualism. The fruits of this individualism are now clear: there are people sleeping in shop doorways, record crime figures, an ever-growing number of single parent families, a jammed housing market and the ascendancy of intolerance.

We can be thankful that the pendulum is starting to swing the other way. Without cooperation, without love of our fellow man, there is nothing in life but the acquisition of material things by fair means or foul, while the disadvantaged try to acquire material wealth through crime. Workers are placed on disadvantageous contracts which makes life precarious. Work is not something we enjoy any longer: the boss regards his employees as expendable while the worker regards his boss with ever growing resentment. Life becomes a struggle, and a once well-ordered society divides into two parts: one trying prise wealth away from the other part who is trying to hold onto it. Seen in the context of our forthcoming afterlives, it is not hard to see that the last decade and a half in Britain has been a serious setback. The afterlife, and our knowledge of it can be a major factor in the task of repairing our broken society.

Although the saying is hackneyed, all you need is love. It is not easy to learn to love; you will spend much time and effort in your next life learning precisely this. In this life, most of us will fail. But don't give up for fear of failure. Only love for others will make us want to do things for others' benefit. Only then will we move on to our next lives leaving this world in a better state than we found it.

APPENDIX A

Comparisons with Spiritualism

It would be a romantic breakthrough if everything we have discovered fitted in with spiritualism. There is plenty of agreement, although there is one major difference.

Below are some of the beliefs of spiritualists. Not all spiritualists accord. This is natural: no two priests, scientists, politicians will agree on anything either. But most spiritualists agree on the main points.

Spiritual Helpers
When a child is born into this world, spiritual guides are assigned on the other side. As we have already discovered through the near death experience, there are several spiritual helpers. Three is a typical figure.

The child may grow up to be a sculptor; one of the spirit guides will be a sculptor, too. This, the spiritualists tell us, is the reason why a child at school might display knowledge of a certain subject far in advance of his age group. For instance, a child chess prodigy might have Capablanca or Steinitz as a spiritual helper, or a child with a genius for physics might have Einstein or Planck.

When our child, with the talent for sculpture, grows up to become a celebrated sculptor and dies, he may want to accept the task of being a spiritual helper to yet another sculptor.

Some spiritualists believe that all the important events in a person's life are known before he is born.

Beings of Light
The spiritualists know about these entities, too. They are referred to as "ribbons" and come in a variety of colours: white ribbons are "pure"; blue ones are "wonderful"; while black ones are "deadly".

The spiritualists are, like us, of the opinion that ribbons are senior entities and that all of us will eventually become ribbons.

After Death
Often a person who has died has been ill for a long time. Once they have crossed the boundary into the next life, they are taken to a hospital to rest. This is apparently a *real* hospital with doctors and nurses. There the spiritual body is fully healed.

This doesn't seem to agree very well with the accounts of the near death experiencers, who tell us that the spirit body seems to be in the pink, even if the earthly body is not in so good a state. However, since the near death experiencer doesn't cross into the next life, he is not to know exactly what happens next. And, while the spiritual body seems to be in healthy state when compared to the earthly body, that doesn't mean it is in the peak of condition.

Once we are out of this hospital we can be assigned work. Everybody has a job to do. We also spend our time learning. There is plenty to learn – probably all the secrets of the Multiverse.

We each have a partner on the other side – the equivalent of a lover on this side. It might be the same partner we had in our earthly life; it might

be someone else.
Everybody works progressively towards brighter and brighter light.

The Other Side

The world beyond is as real to its inhabitants as this world is to us. Whereas the spiritual body is invisible here, it is very real in the world beyond.

The next world has trees, flowers, rivers, towns, cities – just about everything that is found here.

There is no day, no night. There is no time at all: everything is a perpetual *now*, where past, present and future are interlocked.

We are free to do as we wish; but most spirits choose to work (for no money!) since the purpose of this (our current) life, as well as the next life, is to learn to cooperate with others.

There are many "levels" of the next world. We can reach some of the lower levels during sleep when we dream. Lower levels contain people who are too attached to the Earth. Some people who have been selfish during their lives can create "spheres" for themselves where they are living in worlds of their own.

No one is forced to do anything, but only cooperation will give access to higher levels.

The Purpose of Our Life Here

This life, say the spiritualists is a testing ground where we are allowed to taste all sorts of things, both good and bad.

Some spiritualists say that we possibly actually

choose our selves before we are born, that each self is chosen in order to learn a variety of lessons for our spiritual development. Some spiritualists say that our current lives are not our first existences – that we have been alive in other worlds before.

There are several principles that apply to this world as well as the next. One is that we are all capable of overcoming or at least coping with any problem thrown at us. "We are never given a cross to bear without the strength to bear it." A second principle, which applies even more to the next world than it applies to this one is "like attracts like". This may not mean much when we look at the behaviour of magnets, but it certainly applies to the rest of life. If we are selfish or wicked, we attract loneliness, or like-minded people, or evil spirits. But if we are kind, caring, we will then attract benevolent people and benevolent spirits.

Suicide
Some religions teach that suicide is the unforgivable sin. This flies in the face of Christian essence – that the sad circumstances which caused the suicide to take his life are to be pitied rather than condemned, and that *any* sin is forgivable.

Suicides, say the spiritualists, are taken to a place where they continue to face the very problems which led them to their deaths. For instance, if a widower killed himself because he could not face life without his wife, he would not be allowed to meet her again. The place where suicides are taken is temporary, and they are allowed into the next life proper after they have been corrected.

Hell
This is the only major parting of the ways. The spiritualists say that the only hell there is is the hell we create for ourselves on Earth.

Reincarnation
It might be possible, but it is definitely not the norm.

Love and Knowledge
Here the near death experiencers, the Raudive voices and the spiritualists are in total agreement.

APPENDIX B

The Science in *Breakthrough* – a Reappraisal

It would have been terrific if there had been lots of scientific research following the publication of Raudive's classic, *Breakthrough*. But there hasn't. The main reasons for this inertia have been the sceptical world of the orthodox scientist, and the general lack of interest among both fringe scientists and pseudoscientists.

It therefore behoves me to look at advances in other fields made since the publication of *Breakthrough*. The place to look is the world of physics: not only is it my own specialist field of science; but because physics overlaps with all other sciences, which is why it is called "the Queen of Sciences." At an atomic level, physics overlaps with chemistry; when explaining how the eye works, physics overlaps with biology; when studying the electronic voice phenomenon, physics overlaps with thanatology.

The certainty of life after death, and the means of its proof, will certainly have an effect on some major scientific theories. There have also been some odd pieces of research that may throw some light on how the afterlife works. It is perhaps reassuring to the sceptic, if not the physicist, that the worlds that are still to come all obey laws of physics.

Parallel Worlds
The popular notion of parallel worlds is that they start – in the opinion of some, they finish – in the realms of science fiction, having begun life in a story by H.G.Wells. In fact, the other worlds

notion seems to be a lot older. For instance, ancient Celtic belief and mythology mentions an Otherworld, which is inhabited by the dead of this world. The Otherworld was said to be on Earth. Many early Celtic legends take place in this other realm. The early Arthurian Welsh poem, *The Spoils of Annwn*, features a sea voyage to the Otherworld in search of a magic cauldron – a probable precursor of the Holy Grail. Again in Arthurian mythology, King Arthur, after being mortally wounded at the Battle of Camlann, is taken by boat to the Isle of Avalon. (Some near death experiencers say that the next world is across a stretch of water and is reached by boat, as an alternative to going through a tunnel.) Avalon – Avallach or Aballach are other forms – gets its name from a Gaelic word meaning "rich in apples". This may tempt some, who have heard descriptions of the next world's wonderful gardens to think that Avalon and the world of the near death experiencer are the same. Perhaps they are. We simply don't know how much the ancient Celts and their Druidic shamans knew about life after death. However, since *The Egyptian Book of the Dead* and *The Tibetan Book of the Dead* show that the near death experience was known to these ancients, it might also have been known to the Celts.

The parallel worlds theory began to receive some scientific respectability in the 1950s when the physicist Hugh Everett suggested it as a solution to a quantum mechanical problem that was – and still is – baffling physicists.

If any electromagnetic beam is shone through a double slit, a series of vertical bars arranged side by side - called an interference pattern - appears on a screen placed on the other side of the slits.* When single electrons are fired at the double slits one by one, each electron might go through one slit or the other. Gradually, they will form an interference pattern on the screen. Each electron seems to "know" which slit to go through. How?

Everett's solution is that there is an infinite number of parallel worlds (known as superspace). In this plane, the electron might travel through the right hand slit, but there will be at least one parallel world where the electron will go through the left hand slit.

Other physicists have developed Everett's suggestion from the microscopic world to the macroscopic world. Imagine you are in a self-service cafeteria. You have the choice between two sandwiches: cheese or ham. Two parallel worlds are created (or four or six or more). In one parallel world - or one set of parallel worlds - you choose cheese, in the other ham. You push the tray further towards the cash register. You have a choice of drink. In one parallel world you have tea, in another coffee, in another Coca Cola, in yet another Sprite etc. There may be still more parallel worlds where the cashier overcharges or undercharges.

These ideas are actually being bandied about by orthodox scientists; and yet they are so outlandish that they are actually on a par with the ideas of those who believe in astrology, palmistry etc.

*Called Young's experiment.

And like the outlandish ideas of pseudoscience, there has never been any hard evidence for Everett's superspace. Indeed, what we have discovered would seem to point away from superspace.

Antimatter and Antiworlds
"Raudive, antiwelten sind," which is German for "Raudive, antiworlds are," is one of the most significant messages received by Raudive and quoted in *Breakthrough*. A magazine article by the physicist Holger Ess is included in *Breakthrough* as an appendix. In it Ess echoes the suggestion of Columbia University's Dr. Leon Ledermann that there is an antimatter world existing next to ours, where time travels in a backwards direction. Ess goes on to speculate that this antimatter world is inhabited by the dead of our world.

There is no doubt that antimatter exists. Antiparticles have been detected and made by particle physicists. Some are being kept right now in laboratories, trapped in magnetic fields. Antiparticles can be formed into antimatter. The simplest form of matter is the hydrogen atom. This consists of a proton nucleus and one orbiting electron. As you can have a hydrogen atom, you can have an antihydrogen atom, consisting of an antiproton nucleus with an orbiting antielectron (positron). Antiatoms, such as antideuteron and antihelium have already been constructed in laboratories.

All fundamental particles – with the exception of the photon and the pion π^0, which are their own antiparticles – have a corresponding antiparticle. When a particle and its antiparticle touch each other they annihilate one another and vanish in an explosion of radiation. Ess speculates that the pair of particles may move into the antiworld. This all sounds very well, but we know from our own observations that when someone dies, there is no sudden blast of gamma rays and neutrinos.

As stated, Ess and Ledermann speculate that in an antiworld time would go backwards. *Breakthrough* also contains a suggestion by the Latvian Church pastor, Voldermars A. Rolle, that at the point of death, the part of us that survives is "pure energy" which can travel in straight lines beyond the speed of light. This might fit in with the general notion among physicists that if anything travels faster than light, time would then start to travel backwards.

But before we jump to the conclusion that the next world is made out of antimatter, we should look at another significant message received by Raudive: *"Laika te nav"* (Latvian: "There's no time here.") This message agrees with the recollections of the near death experiencers. The spiritualists also state that there is no time as we know it in the next world. Indeed, if time goes backwards in an antiworld, if a near death experiencer visited an antiworld, he could possibly come back *before* he has died. That has never happened. What has happened, though, is that a long experience has been fitted into about thirty seconds. This would suggest that the next world is indeed timeless.

So how do we fit antimatter in?

All the indications are that the universe we

inhabit comprises of matter and not antimatter. This is absolutely essential because of the annihilation: consider antimatter rain causing your house to disappear.

The prevalent cosmological theory, the Big Bang Theory, where the Universe is expanding from the origin of an infinitely dense point of singularity, has little or no rôle for antimatter to play. The biggest piece of evidence for the Big Bang is the spectrums of faraway galaxies. The light received from them on Earth is shifted towards the red end of the spectrum. This tells us that the galaxies appear to be moving away from us: if they were blueshifted they would be moving towards us. The further away the galaxy, the greater the reshift.

The Big Bang theory, however, is in serious trouble. New information from the Hubble Telescope in outer space has almost killed the theory. For instance, the furthest-flung, and thus the oldest, galaxies contain far too many young blue stars. This would tend to suggest these galaxies are younger rather than older. There are other problems, the most celebrated being that according to calculations, most of the matter in the Universe isn't there. This has brought about the Dark Matter Theory. Scientists have spent years searching for this dark matter. None has been found; probably because there is none to find.

Waiting in the wings, to take over from the Big Bang, is Hannes Alfvén's Theory of Plasma*

---

*A gas heated to such an extent that atoms are split into their component ions. Examples are the Sun and fire.

Cosmology, which was brilliantly analysed by Alfvén's disciple, Eric J. Lerner, in his book *The Big Bang Never Happened*. In this theory, the Universe is open, infinite and constantly creating itself, superclusters of galaxies being formed from gigantic plasmic clouds. Minature plasmic filaments, from which the galactic superclusters are formed, have been produced in laboratories.

The observed galactic redshift, on which the Big Bang Theory rests, is dealt with by Alvén, by the use of antimatter. According to the great Swedish plasmologist, matter and antimatter are produced simultaneously in equal quantities from the plasmic filament. There follows a period when the edges of matter and antimatter galaxies annihilate each other. Then matter and antimatter both develop protective "crusts" called Leidenfrost layers. From then on, matter and antimatter repel each other, causing the expansion indicated by the galactic redshift.

If there is an antimatter universe lying alongside this one, then, unless it is a negative copy of this one, the evidence we have does not sit very well with the Theory of Plasma Cosmology. This is what I mentioned in the Introduction to this book. We have started with accounts of people who have recounted experiences while "dead" on the operating table and mysterious voices on tape, and we have developed their ramifications until they gnaw at the dying Big Bang Theory's most probable successor.

But the Theory of Plasma Cosmology, which is probably essentially correct, can be saved, even if all Alfvén's precious antimatter is tipped into a parallel universe. There is the "tired light" theory which suggests that the Universe is not expanding, but is static or near static. The galactic redshift is caused by the immense distances the light has to travel.

Of course, the Theory of Plasma Cosmology, like almost all cosmology theories only allows for one Universe. As is becoming increasingly clear, we live not in a universe but in a multiverse. There is nothing at all wrong with a one-dimensional model: it is the scientific method to form simple models to start with. Modern cosmology began when the Dutch Professor of Astronomical Studies, Willem de Sitter, modelled a relativistic universe...that didn't have a thing in it! Gradually, other scientists elaborated de Sitter's empty universe. In due course, Alfvén's single universe theory will be elaborated to include other universes.

Thomas C. Lethbridge
There is little in the way of orthodox experimental work to suggest the existence of parallel universes. There is some highly irregular work by a British retired archaeologist. His scientific instrument was a pendulum (i.e. he used dowsing). This would normally be an excuse to laugh and turn the other way. However, Lethbridge, with his archaeologist's orderliness, measured everything and recorded everything, publicising the fruits of his toil in books like *A Step in the Dark* and *The Power of the Pendulum*. What attracts my attention most of all is the results he arrived at, which startlingly agree with the near death experience accounts, the Raudive

voices and even spiritualism.

With diligent experimentation with his pendulum, Lethbridge discovered that various lengths of pendulum corresponded to materials. In this way, Lethbridge claimed he was able to use his pendulum to find buried items, such as underground streams, underground pipes and truffles. The length forty inches (101.6 cm) corresponded with death. Beyond forty inches, Lethbridge's pendulum would register water, truffle's etc. at the same length plus forty inches. Furthermore, when less than forty inches, the pendulum registered directly above the object. When greater than forty inches, the pendulum was slightly askew, which suggested diffraction.

Faced with this and his subsequent results, Lethbridge began to arrive at the conclusion that his pendulum was registering another dimension. Since it was above the forty-inch measurement for death, he reasoned that this was the afterlife. The pendulum registered flowing time in this dimension, but in Lethbridge's new dimension *there was no time.*

Lethbridge used a longer pendulum to see what would happen after eighty inches. Yes, there was a third dimension. By climbing a flight of stairs and swinging the pendulum from the bannisters, Lethbridge found yet another dimension beyond one hundred and twenty inches. Technical difficulties prevented him from looking for more dimensions.

An interesting calculation of Lethbridge's is the "rate of vibration" of this world and the world he found above forty inches. Using the results he obtained with his pendulum, he calculated that the frequencies of the vibrations in the world beyond were about four times faster than the frequencies here. This might seem odd to many people. But quantum mechanically, where our planet could be regarded as a wave packet, it can make sense. Lethbridge reasoned that the higher frequency explained why the new dimensions he had found were invisible.

When Two Worlds Collide
If Lethbridge's frequency hypothesis is right, it might also explain why Raudive voices seem bound by strange rhythmns.

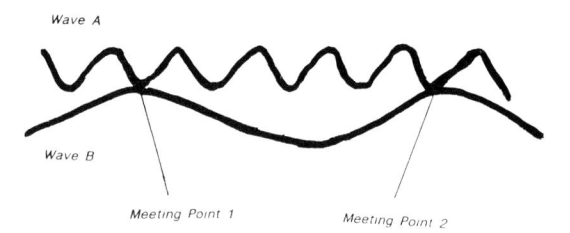

Consider the above diagram.
Wave A has a frequency four times that of Wave B. Because of this, the two waves only meet at Meeting Point 1 and Meeting Point 2. If the dead are communicating from the world beyond onto a tape recorder, a voice can only be put on tape at those meeting points. Of course, the diagram is the simplest possible. The wave variations of the two worlds will look nothing like this; but the principle remains the same.

Theodor Rudolph, Raudive's electrical engineer

friend, deduced that the voices were arriving from the high frequency range. Peter Bander's Great Dane reacted during recording sessions as though he could hear the voices. (My own corgi, on the other hand, lies docilely on the floor as though nothing is happening.)

Robert Monroe
In the 1950s, Robert Monroe, an American businessman, claimed to have had a series of out-of-the-body experiences. Like Lethbridge, I would normally give such an account a wide berth were his results not so near to what we now know that they can't be ignored.

In his book, *Journey Out of the Body*, Monroe claims to have visited three dimensions during the wanderings of his astral body. The first thing he noticed once he was out of his earthly body was that the astral body was very uncomfortable at heights near to the ground, but was in its element higher up. This corresponds to the recollections of the near death experiencers who often find themselves initially looking down on their bodies from a point on the ceiling.

Monroe calls our dimension Locale I. The astral body, when it was bored with travelling around Locale I, moved on to Locale II. This was a dimension of thought where his innnermost thoughts were known to everyone else in that locale. (This again equates with the accounts of near death experiencers.

After several explorations of Locale II, Monroe shed his astral body like the second stage of a rocket. His new body moved on to Locale III. There Monroe met his counterself and merged with him. Locale III was a strange world, which Monroe suggested *was made of antimatter*. People travelled about on reclining quadrocycles and wagons were being pulled by a kind of steam locomotive that travelled on roads. There was no electricity. Well, there wouldn't be in an antimatter world: to make electrical current you need electrons!

Conclusions
Since orthodox physics is nowhere near concrete research into parallel worlds that are our post death destiny, we must turn to oddball research. The results achieved by the work of Lethbridge and Monroe are so close to what we have found out by the near death experience and by the electronic voice phenomenon that it is tempting to accept them.

Instead the work of Lethbridge and Monroe only point a direction for us to search. Lethbridge's experiments with the pendulum may be repeatable, but a forty inch plus string and a slight diffraction do not make a series of parallel worlds. But my gut feeling, together with the knowledge I have discovered tells me Lethbridge is mostly correct. The dead are among us and yet nowhere to be seen; they can talk to us and yet cannot be heard; their world is our world and it is somewhere else.

SELECT BIBLIOGRAPHY

Gooch, Stanley, *The Paranormal.*
    (Wildwood, 1978)
Iverson, Jeffrey, *In Search of the Dead.*
    (B.B.C. Books, 1992)
Lerner, Eric J, *The Big Bang Never Happened.*
    (Simon & Schuster, 1992)
Lethbridge, T. C. *A Step in the Dark.*
    (Routledge & Kegan Paul, 1967)
Lethbridge, T.C. *The Power of the Pendulum.*
    (Routledge & Kegan Paul, 1976)
Monroe, Robert, *Journey Out of the Body.*
    (Souvenir, 1972)
Moody, Raymond, *Life After Life.*
    (Bantam, 1980)
Moody, Raymond, *The Light Beyond.*
    (Macmillan, 1988)
O'Brien, Stephen, *Life After Death.*
    (Voices Management, 1990)
    (Audio cassette)
Randles, Jenny, *The Afterlife: an Investigation*
    (Piatkus, 1993)
Raudive, Konstantin, *Breakthrough.*
    (Colin Smythe, 1971)
Wilson, Colin, *Mysteries.*
    (Granada, 1979)

Alfvén, Hannes, 86-87
animal spirits, 33
antimatter, 84-87, 92
antiworlds, 84-85, 92
Arthur, king, 82
atheists, 11, 67, 69-70
Avalon, 82

Bander, Peter, 43, 91
Barrett, Sir William, 13
beings of light, 15-17,
   49, 71
big bang theory, 86-87
brain, 22, 27
Breakthrough, 23-26, 38,
   43, 63, 81
Buddha, 16
Bullen, Anne, 61

Caesar, Julius, 49, 61
Camlann, battle of, 82
Capablanca, José Raoul, 76
capital punishment, 64-65
Catholicism, 53, 58-59, 69
Celtic Otherworld, 82
Child Support Agency, 71
Churchill, Sir Winston,
   24, 49
Christ, Jesus, 10, 16,
   50, 54
Copperfield, David, 8

Daniels, Paul, 8
dark matter, 86

Desmond Dekker & the
   Aces, 41
Do Det Ike, 25, 42
Dr. Who 53-54
Dostoyevski, Fyodor, 63-64,
   73

Edison, Thomas, 67-68
Egyptian Book of the Dead,
   14, 82
Einstein, Albert, 76
electronic voice phenomenon,
   5, 23-58, 63, 73-74,
   80-81
Elijah, 49
Ellis, David, 40-41, 44
English language, 43-44
Ess, Holger, 84-85
Everett, Hugh, 82-83

Gallup, 17
goniometer, 39
Gooch, Stanley, 41, 44
grand unified field theory,
   5

Heaven, 59
Hell, 47-48, 53-55, 59, 69,
   80
Hitler, Adolf, 48-49
Holy Grail, 82

Israelites, The, 41-42
In Search of the Dead, 24
Iverson, Jeffrey, 24

Index

John-Paul II, Pope, 21
Jürgenson, Friedrich, 23, 28, 33, 36, 38, 42-43, 48, 64

Kasparov, Garry, 52
Keating, Fred, 60
Kennedy, John F, 24
knowledge, 47-48, 50-52, 80

Latvian language, 42-45
Ledermann, Dr. Leon, 84-85
Lerner, Eric J, 87
Lethbridge, Thomas C, 88-92
life review, 15, 66-67
love, 17, 46, 48-51, 75, 80

Mary, Queen of Scots, 61-62
Meek, George, 11
Monroe, Robert, 91-92
Moody, Dr. Raymond, 13, 15, 17-19, 21
multiverse, 47, 70, 77

National Socialist (Nazi) Party 48,
near death experiences, 5, 13-22, 46-50, 58, 62, 66, 71-72, 74, 80
negative near death experiences, 48, 56
Newton, Sir Isaac, 5, 10, 12

O'Neil, Bill, 11
ouija boards, 11, 65
out-of-the-body experiences, 19-20, 91-92

parallel worlds, 52, 81-82, 89-91
Pearson, Ronald, 12
planchettes, 65
Planck, Max, 76
plasma cosmology theory, 86-88
Pope, Alexander, 51
Power of the Pendulum, The, 88
Purgatory, 58-59
psychokinesis, 46
Pye Studios, 44

Quakers, 67
quantum mechanics, 5, 12-13, 90

Raudive, Dr. Konstantin, 23, 26-29, 32-34, 36-39, 42-45, 49-50, 57-58, 63, 73, 81, 88
regression, 60-62
reincarnation, 9, 14, 60-63
relativistic mechanics, 5, 12
Rolle, Voldermans A, 85
Rudolph, Theodor, 39, 90

St. Paul, 70
de Sitter, Willem, 88
spirit helpers, 47, 62, 76
spiritual (astral) body, 14-16, 33, 49, 77
spiritualism, 12, 53, 76-80
Spoils of Annwn, 82
Steinitz, Wilhelm, 76
Step in the Dark, A, 88
subconscious, 46, 62
suicide, 47, 70-72, 79-80
Swedish language, 42-43

Tibetan Book of the Dead, 13-14, 82
thanatology, 6, 81
Tolstoi, Count Lyov, 49
"tunnel" experiences, 15, 22, 49
Tutenkhamen, 49

universe, 47, 70, 74, 86

Wells, HG, 81
Wilson, Colin, 62, 76

Young's experiment, 82-83